J. Dassow

Completeness Problems in the Structural Theory of Automata

Mathematical Research · Mathematische Forschung

Wissenschaftliche Beiträge
herausgegeben von der
Akademie der Wissenschaften der DDR
Institut für Mathematik

Band 7

Completeness Problems in the Structural Theory of Automata

by
J. Dassow

Completeness Problems in the Structural Theory of Automata

by
Jürgen Dassow

Akademie-Verlag · Berlin 1981

Verfasser:

Doz. Dr. Jürgen Dassow
Technische Hochschule „Otto von Guericke"
3010 Magdeburg
Boleslav-Bierut-Platz 5

Die Titel dieser Schriftenreihe werden vom Originalmanuskript der Autoren reproduziert.

Erschienen im Akademie-Verlag, DDR-1080 Berlin, Leipziger Str. 3—4
Lektor: Dr. Reinhard Höppner

Lizenznummer: 202 · 100/423/81
Gesamtherstellung: VEB Kongreß- und Werbedruck, 9273 Oberlungwitz
Umschlag: Rolf Kunze
Bestellnummer: 762 951 9 (2182/7) · LSV 1025
Printed in GDR
DDR 20,— M

To Christine

PREFACE

Nowadays there are numerous monographs on automata theory or on special aspects of automata theory. However, the completeness problem of structural theory, whether or not any automaton mapping can be realized by an arbitrarily given set of elementary automaton mappings, is not included or only the main results are presented. On the other hand, in recent years there have been published some monographs and survey papers on the completeness problem for functions over a finite set, which correspond to combinational automata. The aim of this book is to fill up this gap. It presents a survey of the results on completeness in algebras of sequential functions and some special subclasses.

The book is self-contained. All necessary fundamental concepts and facts are introduced, but familiarity of the reader with foundations of algebra, automata theory, etc. will be helpful. The purpose of the exercises is a two-fold one. The reader can check his knowledge, and some of them give additional new information.

The presentation is purely mathematical. The monograph turns mainly to mathematicians and computer scientists, but it can also be of interest for engineers working in design of automata.

I want to express my gratitude to V.A.Buevic (Moscow), G.Burosch, D.Lau, W.Rathay (Rostock), H.Reichel (Magdeburg), and B.Thalheim (Dresden) for many discussions on the subject and/or for their remarks on a preliminary version. I wish to thank my wife for her careful help in producing the final copy. Finally, I also want to acknowledge Akademie-Verlag, especially R.Höppner, for friendly co-operation and including this publication in series "Mathematical Research".

Magdeburg, March 1981 Jürgen Dassow

CONTENTS

INTRODUCTION

Besides the abstract theory of automata (including e.g. minimization, acceptance of sets of words, experiments) and algebraic theory (relations between automata and semigroups), one of the main parts of automata theory is the structural theory which discusses the realization of an automaton by simpler automata. Its purpose is to model some general working mechanisms of certain parts of the hardware of real automata. It can contribute to solve some special problems of the design of automata or can give a mathematical understanding of the heuristic methods used in practice (see /Gl/, /Jac/).
The structural theory of automata consists of decomposition and synthesis theory,which is sometimes also called theory of logical nets. The problem of decomposition is as follows: Given an automaton, decompose it in smaller (simpler) automata. There are different theories according to the measure of simplicity, e.g. the number of states (see /HS/, /No4/) or the complexity of associated semigroups (see /Ar/). The synthesis deals with the converse problem: Given a set of simple elementary automata which correspond to gates, chips, etc., construct a more complicated automaton. Here, we have to answer the following questions:

- Completeness Problem: Which automata can be constructed from a given set of elementary automata? Find an algorithm to construct a given automaton. Give some conditions which ensure that we can realize all input-output-behaviours (of a certain type).
- Minimization: Find algorithms to construct a minimal realization of a given automaton by the elementary automata, for instance a realization with a minimal number of elementary automata, etc. (see /Mi/, /DDT/). Determine bounds on the complexity of optimal realizations (/Tr1/).
- Realization with additional properties: Find such sets of elementary automata and a corresponding realization of an automaton such that it is easy to detect faults (/Hay/, /Coy/, /Re/, /Gö/), or hazards are avoided or easily to detect (/Ei/, /Un/), or the realization has a regular structure (/He/, /ANT/). With each of these realizations we can also associate a special completeness problem.

In this monograph we consider only the completeness problem with respect to a given class of automata and a given class of connections of the elementary automata. Especially we are interested in the following two aspects:

- Find a criterion for completeness of a set M of elementary auto-

mata, i.e. find a criterion whether or not any automaton of the given class can be constructed from M using the given connections.
- Give an algorithm to decide whether or not M is complete.

Therefore we shall not consider such classes of automata and connections where we have only examples of complete sets or investigations on examples. For instance, this is often the cases with respect to the problems of realizations with additional properties. Note that each decomposition theory leads to an example of a complete set.

The representation of the material is purely mathematical. We shall regard the class of automata as the underlying set of an algebra whose operations correspond to the connections. Then the completeness problem coincides with the problem of generation of the underlying set by its subsets.

Mostly, we consider the algebra $\underline{P_k}$ where the underlying set consists of sequential functions, i.e. functions induced by finite automata or logical nets, and the operations are formalized connections of logical nets. The exact definition is given in Chapter 2. In Chapter 4 we study its properties with respect to the completeness problem. We prove that $\underline{P_k}$ is finitely generated, give a general completeness criterion and show that there is no algorithm deciding the completeness of a finite set. The latter result is the motive to modify the completeness concept. We want to generate only a representative subset of the underlying set instead of the whole underlying set or we take only special sets as system of generators. Five such modifications are considered in Chapter 5. Three of them have an undecidable completeness problem, too; for the other two modifications, there is an algorithm which decides the completeness.

The Chapters 3, 6, 7 are devoted to special subalgebras or to slight modifications of the operations. We consider algebras of functions over a finite set, sequential functions which are induced by automata with the same input and output set, delayed functions, and functions associated with register machines. We obtain different properties with respect to the same problems. Therefore these results contribute to a better understanding of the completeness problem in $\underline{P_k}$.

1. FUNDAMENTAL CONCEPTS

1.1. Universal Algebra

The subject of this monograph is the study of functions which are induced by finite automata and operations which are applied to such functions in order to obtain new functions. Since we shall sometimes make restrictions on the automata or the operations, we shall first give such concepts and results which will hold independent of these restrictions and which are useful for our purposes. For more detailed information on the algebraic foundations we refer to /Co/ and /Ce1/.

A universal algebra $\underline{A}$ is a construct $\underline{A} = (A;\Omega)$, where A is a nonempty set and Ω is a family of finitary operations

$$f_i : A^{n_i} \longrightarrow A, \ i \in I.$$

If f_i is 0-ary, f_i distinguishes an element of A. A is called the underlying set of $\underline{A}$ or the carrier of $\underline{A}$. Notice that the operations of Ω can also be partial operations. If the set of operations is known from the context, then the carrier of $\underline{A}$ is denoted by A, and conversely, $\underline{A}$ denotes the algebra with carrier A.

Example 1.1. i) $\underline{\mathbb{Z}} = (\mathbb{Z}; +, -)$ has the underlying set $\mathbb{Z}$ of integers and the operations are addition and subtraction.

ii) Let $\mathbb{R}^n$ denote the set of n-dimensional row-vectors whose components are real numbers. Let $+$ denote the usual vector addition, and for $\alpha \in \mathbb{R}$ let c_α be the unary mapping from $\mathbb{R}^n$ in $\mathbb{R}^n$ given by

$$c_\alpha(\underline{a}) = \alpha \underline{a} \quad \text{(multiplication by scalars).}$$

Then

$$\underline{\mathbb{R}}^n = (\mathbb{R}^n; +, (c_\alpha)_{\alpha \in \mathbb{R}})$$

is a universal algebra.

iii) The set $\mathbb{P}$ of polynomials

$$p(x) = a_n x^n + a_{n-1} x^{n-1} + \dots + a_1 x + a_0$$

over $\mathbb{R}$, i.e. $a_i \in \mathbb{R}$ for $i = 0,1,\dots,n$, with the operations $+$ and c_α forms a universal algebra

$$\underline{\mathbb{P}} = (\mathbb{P}; +, (c_\alpha)_{\alpha \in \mathbb{R}}).$$

Special classes of universal algebras are often characterized by some axioms which are required for the operations. We need the concepts of a semigroup and a group.
A semigroup is a universal algebra $\underline{G} = (G;\sigma)$ where the domain of σ is G^2 and the law of associativity holds, i.e.

$$(a\sigma b)\sigma c = a\sigma(b\sigma c).$$

A group is a semigroup which satisfies the following additional axioms
- there is an element $e \in G$ such that

$$a\sigma e = e\sigma a = a$$

  holds for all $a \in G$,
- for any element $a \in G$, there is an element $a^{-1} \in G$ such that

$$a\sigma a^{-1} = a^{-1}\sigma a = e.$$

Let B be a subset of A. $\underline{B} = (B; (g_i)_{i\in I})$ is a subalgebra of $\underline{A} = (A; (f_i)_{i\in I})$, written as $\underline{B} \leq \underline{A}$, iff

i) the arity of f_i and g_i coincide for all $i \in I$,

ii) for $b_1, b_2, \ldots, b_{n_i} \in B$, $g_i(b_1, b_2, \ldots, b_{n_i})$ is defined iff $f_i(b_1, b_2, \ldots, b_{n_i})$ is defined, and if both values are defined, then

$$g_i(b_1, b_2, \ldots, b_{n_i}) = f_i(b_1, b_2, \ldots, b_{n_i}).$$

Hence we can regard g_i as the restriction of f_i on B, and in the sequel we shall use the same notation for the operations in $\underline{B}$ and $\underline{A}$.

Example 1.2. i) For $a \in \mathbb{N}$, let $U_a = \{ia : i \in \mathbb{Z}\}$. Then $\underline{U_a}$ is a subalgebra of $\underline{\mathbb{Z}}$. It can be proved that any subalgebra of $\underline{\mathbb{Z}}$ has the form $\underline{U_a}$.

ii) The subalgebras of $\underline{\mathbb{R}}^n$ correspond to the vector subspaces of $\underline{\mathbb{R}}^n$ in the sense of linear algebra.

iii) For any $n \in \mathbb{N}$, the polynomials of degree $\leq n$ and the polynomial p with $p(x) = 0$ form a subalgebra of $\underline{\mathbb{P}}$.

For a subset B of the underlying set A of the algebra $\underline{A} = (A;\Omega)$

we define

$$[B]_{\underline{A}} = \bigcap_{\substack{C \supseteq B \\ \underline{C} \leq \underline{A}}} C .$$

If the algebra $\underline{A}$ is known from the context, we only write $[B]$ instead of $[B]_{\underline{A}}$. The following facts follow immediately from the definition. The mapping $B \longrightarrow [B]$ is a closure operator, i.e.

i) $B \subseteq [B]$,

ii) $B_1 \subseteq B_2$ implies $[B_1] \subseteq [B_2]$,

iii) $[[B]] = [B]$.

Since the intersection of subalgebras is a subalgebra, too, $[B]$ is the underlying set of a subalgebra which is denoted by $[\underline{B}]$. Moreover, $[\underline{B}]$ is the smallest subalgebra containing B. Further, $B = [B]$ if and only if $\underline{B}$ is a subalgebra.
Now we give a constructive description of $[B]$. We put $B_0 = B$, and, for $i \geq 1$, let B_i consist of B_{i-1} and all elements $\sigma(a_1, a_2, \ldots, a_n)$ where σ is an n-ary operation of Ω and $a_1, a_2, \ldots, a_n \in B_{i-1}$. We define

$$B' = \bigcup_{i \geq 0} B_i .$$

| <u>Lemma 1.1.</u> $B' = [B]$.

Proof. We prove that $\underline{B'}$ is a subalgebra, and since $B = B_0 \subseteq B'$, we obtain $[B] \subseteq B'$ by definition of $[B]$. Let

$$a_1, a_2, \ldots, a_n \in B',$$

and let σ be an n-ary operation of Ω . Then $a_i \in B_{k_i}$ for some k_i. If

$$k = \max_{1 \leq i \leq n} k_i ,$$

we have

$$\{a_1, a_2, \ldots, a_n\} \subseteq B_k .$$

Then

$$\sigma(a_1, a_2, \ldots, a_n) \in B_{k+1} \subseteq B' .$$

Further we show $B_k \subseteq [B]$ for all $k \geq 0$. In order to prove this it suffices to show that $B_k \subseteq C$ for all subalgebras $\underline{C}$ with $B \subseteq C$. By definition, $B_0 \subseteq C$. Assume that $B_i \subseteq C$ has already been shown, and let $a \in B_{i+1}$. Then $a \in B_i$ or $a = \sigma(a_1, a_2, \ldots, a_n)$ for some $a_1, a_2, \ldots, a_n \in B_i$ and $\sigma \in \Omega$. Since $\underline{C}$ is a subalgebra, we obtain $a \in C$, and thus $B_{i+1} \subseteq C$ is proved.

Therefore we can say that B generates $[B]$.

The following concept is very important because it will be the central notion of this monograph. $M \subseteq A$ is called complete in $\underline{A} = (A;\Omega)$ or a system of generators for $\underline{A}$ iff

$$[M] = A .$$

Let M be complete in $\underline{A}$. We say that M is reducible if and only if there is an element $a \in M$ such that $M \setminus \{a\}$ is complete, too. An irreducible complete set M is called a basis. We say that $\underline{A}$ is finitely generated iff there is a finite set which is complete in $\underline{A}$.

Lemma 1.2. If $\underline{A}$ is finitely generated, then

i) $\underline{A}$ has a basis,

ii) any basis of $\underline{A}$ is finite, and

iii) any complete set can be reduced to a basis.

Proof. Let $M = \{a_1, a_2, \ldots, a_n\}$ be a finite system of generators for $\underline{A}$. Put

$$M_0 = M$$

and define inductively

$$M_{i+1} = \begin{cases} M_i & \text{if } [M_i] \neq [M_i \setminus \{a_i\}] \\ M_i \setminus \{a_i\} & \text{otherwise.} \end{cases}$$

Obviously, M_{n-1} forms a basis.

Now let M' be an arbitrary complete set. Then $\{a_1, a_2, \ldots, a_n\} \subseteq [M']$. In order to generate the elements $a_1, a_2, \ldots, a_n$ we need only a finite number of elements of M', and this finite set of generators can be reduced by the above process.

For a universal algebra $\underline{A} = (A;\Omega)$, therefore one of the following cases holds:

i) $\underline{A}$ is finitely generated,

ii) $\underline{A}$ has no basis, i.e. any complete set is reducible,

iii) any complete set can be reduced to a basis and $\underline{A}$ has no finite basis,

iv) there is no finite basis in $\underline{A}$, there is an infinite basis in $\underline{A}$, and there is a complete set M in A such that any complete subset of M is reducible.

We say that $\underline{A}$ is of type 1,2,3,and 4, respectively.

Example 1.3. i) $\underline{\mathbb{Z}} = (\mathbb{Z};\ +,\ -)$ is finitely generated since $\{1\}$ forms a basis. We observe that there are bases with cardinality $\neq 1$, for instance $\{6,\ 10,\ 15\}$ (we have $6 + 10 - 15 = 1$, and a subset of $\{6,\ 10,\ 15\}$ can generate only multiples of its greatest common divisor $d \neq 1$), moreover, for any number $r \geq 2$, there is a basis for $\underline{\mathbb{Z}}$ consisting of exactly r integers.

ii) $\underline{\mathbb{R}}^n$ has a finite basis, and any basis of $\underline{\mathbb{R}}^n$ consists of n elements.

iii) $\underline{\mathbb{P}}$ is of type 3.

Lemma 1.3. If the algebra $\underline{A} = (A;\Omega)$ is finitely generated, then every chain

$$\underline{B_o} \subseteq \underline{B_1} \subseteq \dots \subseteq \underline{B_n} \subseteq \underline{B_{n+1}} \subseteq \dots \subseteq \underline{A}$$

of subalgebras such that

$$\bigcup_{i\geq 0} B_i = A$$

is a finite chain, i.e. there is a number t such that

$$\underline{B_t} = \underline{B_{t+1}} = \dots = \underline{A}$$

Proof. Let $\{a_1,a_2,\dots,a_n\}$ be a finite system of generators of $\underline{A}$. Since $\bigcup_{i\geq 0} B_i = A$, there are numbers k_i such that $a_i \in B_{k_i}$. Then $\{a_1,a_2,\dots,a_n\} \subseteq B_k$, where $k = \max_{1\leq i\leq n} k_i$, and therefore

$$A = [\{a_1,a_2,\dots,a_n\}] \subseteq B_k \subseteq A\ .$$

This implies

$$\underline{B_k} = \underline{B_{k+1}} = \dots = \underline{A}\ .$$

A subalgebra $\underline{B}$ of $\underline{A}$ is called maximal in $\underline{A}$ if and only if

i) $B \neq A$,

ii) there is no subalgebra $\underline{C}$ such that $\underline{B} \subsetneq \underline{C} \subsetneq \underline{A}$.

Example 1.4. i) The maximal subalgebras of $\underline{Z} = (Z; +, -)$ are given by the underlying sets $U_p = \{ip : i \in Z\}$ where p is a prime number.

ii) The maximal subalgebras of $\underline{\mathbb{R}}^n$ are the (n-1)-dimensional subspaces of $\underline{\mathbb{R}}^n$, i.e. the vector spaces generated by $n - 1$ linearly independent vectors.

iii) A maximal subalgebra of $\underline{\mathbb{P}}$ is formed by the polynomials

$$p(x) = a_n x^n + a_{n-1} x^n + \dots + a_1 x \quad .$$

Lemma 1.4. A subalgebra $\underline{B}$ of $\underline{A}$ is maximal in $\underline{A}$ if and only if the following conditions are satisfied:

i) $B \neq A$,

ii) for each element $a \in A \setminus B$, we have $[B \cup \{a\}] = A$.

Proof. Suppose $\underline{B}$ is maximal. Since $[B] = B$ and $a \notin B$, we have $[B \cup \{a\}] \supsetneq B$, and therefore $A = [B \cup \{a\}]$. If $\underline{B}$ is not maximal, then there is a subalgebra $\underline{C}$ such that $\underline{B} \subsetneq \underline{C} \subsetneq \underline{A}$. Let $a \in C \setminus B$. Then $B \subseteq [B \cup \{a\}] \subseteq C$ and hence $[B \cup \{a\}] \neq A$.

Lemma 1.5. If $\underline{A}$ is finitely generated, then each proper subalgebra of $\underline{A}$ is contained in a maximal subalgebra of $\underline{A}$.

Proof. Let $\underline{B}$ be a proper subalgebra of $\underline{A}$. We define the set $\mathfrak{M}$ as the set of all subalgebras $\underline{C}$ with $\underline{B} \subseteq \underline{C}$ and $\underline{A} \neq \underline{C}$. By Lemma 1.3., any chain in $\mathfrak{M}$ (sets ordered by inclusion) has a lowest upper bound in $\mathfrak{M}$. Using the Lemma of Zorn (see/Hal/), $\mathfrak{M}$ has a maximal element which is a subalgebra with the required property.

Lemma 1.6. Let $\underline{A}$ be finitely generated. Then $M \subseteq A$ is complete in $\underline{A}$ if and only if M is not contained in any maximal subalgebra of $\underline{A}$.

Proof. Assume M is contained in a maximal subalgebra $\underline{B}$ (more precisely in the underlying set of the subalgebra $\underline{B}$). Then $[M] \subseteq B$, and thus M is not complete.
Conversely, if M is not complete, then $[\underline{M}] \neq \underline{A}$, and by Lemma 1.5., $[M]$ is contained in a maximal subalgebra of $\underline{A}$.

Lemma 1.7. If $\underline{A}$ is finitely generated and $|A| \leq \aleph_0$ [1], then there is a countable set $\mathfrak{M}$ of maximal subalgebras of $\underline{A}$ such that a finite set $M \subseteq A$ is complete in $\underline{A}$ if and only if $M \nsubseteq N$ for all $\underline{N} \in \mathfrak{M}$.

Proof. The set $\mathfrak{N}$ of all finite subsets of A which are not complete is countable. For $M' \in \mathfrak{N}$ we can find a maximal subalgebra $\underline{M}''$ of $\underline{A}$ with $M' \subseteq M''$. Then the set $\mathfrak{M}$ of all maximal subalgebras $\underline{M}''$ constructed in this way has the required properties.

Lemma 1.8. The number of maximal subalgebras of $\underline{A}$ is an upper bound for the maximal cardinality of a basis of $\underline{A}$.

Proof. Let M be a basis. For every maximal subalgebra M' there is an element $a_{M'} \in M$ with $a_{M'} \notin M'$, by Lemma 1.6.. Clearly,

$$\{a_{M'} : M' \text{ maximal subalgebra of } \underline{A}\} = N$$

is a system of generators for $\underline{A}$. Since M is a basis, we obtain $M = N$ and therefore the assertion.

A homomorphism h from $\underline{A} = (A; (f_i)_{i \in I})$ onto $\underline{B} = (B; (g_i)_{i \in I})$ is a mapping from A onto B such that

i) for all $i \in I$, g_i and f_i have the same arity, say n_i,

ii) $f_i(a_1, a_2, \ldots, a_{n_i})$ is defined if and only if

$g_i(h(a_1), h(a_2), \ldots, h(a_{n_i}))$ is defined, and

iii) if both values are defined, then

$$h(f_i(a_1, a_2, \ldots, a_{n_i})) = g_i(h(a_1), h(a_2), \ldots, h(a_{n_i})) .$$

An isomorphism is a one-to-one homomorphism. If the set Ω of operations of the algebra $\underline{A}$ contains an n-ary operation σ which is non-defined for all elements of A^n, then we shall also say that $\underline{A}$ and $\underline{A}' = (A, \Omega \setminus \{\sigma\})$ are isomorphic.

---

[1] As usual, we denote by $|X|$ the cardinality of the set X and by $\aleph_0$ the cardinality of the set of integers.

1.2. Algorithm Theory

For many problems, there arise two special problems:

i) Does there exist a solution of the problem?

ii) Does there exist an algorithm which produces the solution?

We know that, for any two given integers, there exist their greatest common divisor, and the Euclidean algorithm is one of the methods which determines this integer. A lot of criteria whether or not a system of linear equations is solvable are known, and if a solution exists, then we can compute it by the Gaussian algorithm, for instance. Any formula can be regarded as an algorithm in order to determine the solution of a problem, for instance the solutions of a cubic equation can be calculated by the formula of Cardano.
In modern mathematics, algorithms play an important role since a lot of problems can be solved only by the use of a computer, and computers can only work with algorithms.
The algebraic concept of completeness of the preceding paragraph has also an algorithmic aspect. Let $\underline{A}$ be a finitely generated universal algebra, and let M be a finite subset of A. We ask whether or not M is complete in $\underline{A}$. If we consider the algebra

$$\underline{\mathbb{R}}^n = (\mathbb{R}^n; +, (c_\alpha)_{\alpha \in \mathbb{R}})$$

defined in Example 1.1. and a subset $M \subseteq \mathbb{R}^n$, M is complete if and only if M consists of n linearly independent elements of $\mathbb{R}^n$.
By definition, $\underline{a}_1, \underline{a}_2, \ldots, \underline{a}_n$ are linearly independent if and only if the system

$$\alpha_1 \underline{a}_1 + \alpha_2 \underline{a}_2 + \ldots + \alpha_n \underline{a}_n = \underline{0}$$

of linear equations has the unique solution

$$\alpha_1 = \alpha_2 = \ldots = \alpha_n = 0.$$

Using the Gaussian algorithm it can be decided whether or not M generates $\mathbb{R}^n$.
Even in our daily life we often find algorithms. Describing the way to the railway station in a foreign town can be regarded as an algorithm; a recipe is an algorithm to prepare a good roast meat; the operating instructions are an algorithm for handling a new apparatus. All the above algorithms have one thing in common:

1. They consist of a finite number of rules.
2. There is a uniquely determined rule which has to be applied first.
3. If we have applied a rule, then we have a uniquely determined rule which has to be applied as the next rule, or we know that the work of the algorithm is finished.
4. The application of a rule can be done effectively "without" intelligence, for instance by a machine.

Further, any algorithm has some input data (for instance the two numbers whose greatest common divisor has to be determined; sugar, eggs, etc. which are needed for making a cake ; a finite subset of the underlying set of a universal algebra) and "computes" a result (the greatest common divisor, the cake, or the words "yes" or "no").
Sometimes the above question i) can be answered easily by means of an indirect proof or it can be obviously solved, but question ii) is very difficult to answer. For instance, the question whether or not a given real number is algebraic has to have the answer "yes" or "no", but it is very difficult to find the answer. Moreover, we can ask: Does there exist an algorithm to find the solution of a given problem? In order to answer this question precisely we have to give an exact (formal) definition of the concept of an algorithm. This can be done by means of

- Turing machines,
- partially recursive functions,
- Markov normal algorithms,
- (formalized) flow diagrams.

We shall not give such an exact definition and refer to /Ma/, /Kl/, and /Tr2/. For our purposes the above intuitive characterization of an algorithm will be sufficient if we want to prove that there is an algorithm which determines the solution. In case the problem is undecidable, i.e. no such algorithm exists, we give two examples which are needed later. In order to do this we need some foundations about word sets. Therefore we give all related concepts used in this monograph here.

An alphabet X is a finite nonempty set. The elements of X are called letters. A word over X is a finite sequence of letters, written as

$$p = x_1x_2...x_n \text{ , } x_i \in X \text{ for } 1 \leq i \leq n.$$

The length of a word p is the number of letters of p where a letter which occurs t times in p is counted t times, too. Further, we introduce the empty word λ of length 0. The set of all words over X (including λ) is denoted by X^*, and we put $X^+ = X^* \setminus \{\lambda\}$. An ω-word over X is an infinite sequence of letters of X, written as $p = x_1x_2\ldots$. It is called periodic if there exist two integers $t, s > 0$ such that $x_{i+t} = x_i$ for $i \geq s$. t is called the period of p.

The concatenation of the words $p = x_1x_2\ldots x_n$ and $q = y_1y_2\ldots y_m$ is defined as

$$pq = x_1x_2\ldots x_ny_1y_2\ldots y_m .$$

Then $p\cdot\lambda = \lambda\cdot p = p$ for all $p \in X^*$, and if $l(p)$ denotes the length of p, we have $l(pq) = l(p) + l(q)$. For sets $L_1 \subseteq X^*$, $L_2 \subseteq X^*$, we define

$$L_1 \cdot L_2 = \{p_1p_2 : p_1 \in L_1, p_2 \in L_2\} .$$

Further, for $L \subseteq X^*$, we put

$$L^0 = \{\lambda\} ,$$

$$L^{i+1} = L^i . L \quad \text{for} \quad i \geq 0,$$

and

$$L^* = \bigcup_{i \geq 0} L^i .$$

The set of regular sets over X is defined inductively as follows:

i) A finite set $L \subseteq X^*$ is regular.

ii) If L, L_1, $L_2 \subseteq X^*$ are regular, then $L_1 \cup L_2$, $L_1 \cdot L_2$, and L^* are also regular.

iii) $L \subseteq X^*$ is regular if and only if it is regular by i) and ii).

A normal Post algorithm is a triple $A = (X, \mu, \{(x, w_x) : x \in X\})$ where i) X is an alphabet,

ii) $\mu \in \mathbb{N}$, $\mu \geq 1$,

iii) $w_x \in X^*$ for $x \in X$.

We say that $p = x_1x_2\ldots x_n$ directly derives q, written as $p \Rightarrow q$, if and only if

$$n \geq \mu \quad \text{and} \quad q = x_{\mu+1}x_{\mu+2}\ldots x_nw_{x_1} .$$

Then, with any word p we can associate a unique derivation

$$p \Rightarrow p_1 \Rightarrow p_2 \Rightarrow \ldots \quad .$$

We say that p has a finite derivation iff p generates a sequence

$$p = p_0 \Rightarrow p_1 \Rightarrow p_2 \Rightarrow \dots \Rightarrow p_{n-1} \Rightarrow p_n$$

where $n \geq 0$ and $l(p_n) < \mu$, i.e. there is no word which can be derived from p_n. In the opposite case ($l(p_i) \geq \mu$ for all $i \geq 0$) p has an infinite derivation.

<u>Example 1.5.</u> i) We consider

$$A = (\{a,b,c\},\ 2,\ \{(a,a),\ (b,b),\ (c,c^3)\}).$$

Then $(ab)^n$ has the following derivation

$$(ab)^n \Rightarrow (ab)^{n-1}a \Rightarrow (ab)^{n-2}a^2 \Rightarrow \dots \Rightarrow aba^{n-1} \Rightarrow a^n$$

$$\Rightarrow a^{n-2}a = a^{n-1} \Rightarrow a^{n-2} \Rightarrow \dots \Rightarrow a^2 \Rightarrow a .$$

Thus $(ab)^n$ has a finite derivation for all $n \geq 1$. $(ca)^2$ has an infinite derivation because

$$(ca)^2 \Rightarrow cac^3 \Rightarrow c^3c^3 = c^6 \Rightarrow c^4c^3 = c^7 \Rightarrow c^8 \Rightarrow \dots \Rightarrow c^n \Rightarrow \dots .$$

It can be proved that p has an infinite derivation if and only if $p = x_1x_2 \dots x_n$ with $n \geq 2$ and if there is an i such that $x_{2i+1} = c$ and $0 \leq i < n/2$.

ii) If $l(w_x) \geq \mu$ for all $x \in X$, then p has a finite derivation if and only if $l(p) < \mu$.

With each normal Post algorithm A we can associate the function

$$f_A : X^* \rightarrow X^*$$

defined as follows

$$f_A(p) = \begin{cases} \lambda & \text{if } p \text{ has a finite derivation} \\ a & \text{otherwise ,} \end{cases}$$

where a is a fixed element of X. It is proved (see /Ma/) that there is a normal Post algorithm A such that f_A is not partially recursive (or, equivalently, there is no Turing machine which computes $f_A(p)$ for each word p as input), i.e. there is no algorithm which decides whether or not a (arbitrarily) given word p has a finite derivation in A. Notice that it is possible to decide this question for special words by their special structures, but then this method is not applicable to all words, i.e. it does not compute f_A.

A semi-Thue-system over X is a set of productions,

$$T = \{u_1 \rightarrow v_1, u_2 \rightarrow v_2, \ldots, u_n \rightarrow v_n\}$$

where $u_1, u_2, \ldots, u_n \in X^+$, $v_1, v_2, \ldots, v_n \in X^*$. Let $U = \{u_1, u_2, \ldots, u_n\}$. We say that $p \in X^*$ directly derives $q \in X^*$ in T if and only if

i) $p = p_1 u_i p_2$ for some words $p_1, p_2 \in X^*$ and $u_i \in U$ such that u_i is the only subword of $p_1 u_i$ which is contained in U,

ii) $q = p_1 v_i p_2$,

iii) $u_i \rightarrow v_i \in T$.

p derives q if there are words $p_0, p_1, \ldots, p_n$, $n \geq 0$, such that

i) $p = p_0$,

ii) $q = p_n$,

iii) for $i = 0, 1, \ldots, n-1$, p_i directly derives p_{i+1}.

With a semi-Thue-system T we associate the function f_T given by

$$f_T(p,q) = \begin{cases} a & \text{if } p \text{ derives } q \\ \lambda & \text{otherwise}, \end{cases}$$

where a is a fixed element of X, again.

<u>Example 1.6.</u> Let

$$T = \{ab \rightarrow ba\} \text{ over } \{a,b\}$$

and

$$p = a^{n_1} b^{m_1} a^{n_2} b^{m_2} \ldots a^{n_t} b^{m_t}$$

where

$$n_1, m_t \geq 0, \quad n_2, n_3, \ldots, n_t \geq 1, \text{ and } m_1, m_2, \ldots, m_{t-1} \geq 1.$$

Then $f_T(p,q) = a$ if and only if there is an integer r with $1 \leq r \leq t$ such that

$$q = b^{m_1} b^{m_2} \ldots b^{m_r'} a^m b a^n b^{m_r''} a^{n_{r+1}} b^{m_{r+1}} \ldots a^{n_t} b^{m_t}$$

where

$$m + n = n_1 + n_2 + \ldots + n_r, \quad m_r' + m_r'' + 1 = m_r.$$

We need the following statement in the sequel: There is a semi-Thue-system T such that f_T is not computable by a Turing machine, i.e.

there is no algorithm which decides whether or not an arbitrarily given word p derives another arbitrarily given word q. For a proof we refer to /Kl/.

Exercises

1. Prove that the mapping $B \to [B]$ is a closure operator.
2. Show that the intersection of subalgebras is a subalgebra.
3. Consider the algebra $\underline{Z}' = (Z; +)$.
   i) Prove that $\underline{Z}'$ is finitely generated, but that there is no single integer which generates $\underline{Z}'$!
   ii) Characterize the subalgebras and the maximal subalgebras of $\underline{Z}$!
4. Let A be a finite set.
   i) Prove that the set of mappings from A into A forms a semigroup with respect to the composition $\circ$ as operation ($(f \circ g)(x) = f(g(x))$).
   ii) Show that the set of one-to-one mappings from A onto A forms a group with respect to composition.
   iii) Let $A = \{0,1,2,3\}$. Determine a basis for the algebras defined in i) and ii).
5. Let $A = (\{a,b,c\}, 3, \{(a,a^2), (b,b^2), (c,abc)\})$ be a normal Post algorithm. Determine f_A.
6. Let $T = \{a \to c^2, csb \to s^2, s \to asb\}$ be a semi-Thue-system over $\{a,b,c,s\}$. Determine the set of words which can be derived from s.
7. If $\underline{M_i}$, $i \geq 1$, are subalgebras with $\underline{M_j} \subseteq \underline{M_{j+1}}$ for $j \geq 1$, then $\bigcup_{i \geq 1} M_i$ also forms a subalgebra.

2. THE ALGEBRA OF SEQUENTIAL FUNCTIONS

2.1. Sequential Functions, Automata, Logical Nets

In this paragraph we introduce the underlying set of the algebra which will be under consideration in the monograph. We shall give three equivalent definitions. Thus we shall be in a position to use the most appropriate mechanism in the proofs in the following paragraphs, and we obtain also a motivation for the operations of the algebra.

A function $F : X^* \rightarrow Y^*$ is called sequential if and only if the following conditions are satisfied:

i) $l(F(p)) = l(p)$ for all $p \in X^*$,

ii) for every $p \in X^*$, there exists a function F_p such that

$$F(pq) = F(p)F_p(q) \quad \text{for all} \quad q \in X^*,$$

iii) the set $Z_F = \{F_p : p \in X^*\}$ is finite.

The cardinality of Z_F is called the weight of F. Obviously $F_\lambda = F$.

Example 3.1. Let

$$\bar{s} = \begin{cases} 1 & \text{iff } s \text{ is odd} \\ 2 & \text{iff } s \text{ is even,} \end{cases}$$

$X = \{0,1\}^2$, $Y = \{0,1\}$. Then the function F_1 defined by

$$F_1((x_1(1),x_2(1))(x_1(2),x_2(2))\ldots(x_1(t),x_2(t))) = x_1(1)x_2(2)x_1(3)x_2(4)\ldots x_{\bar{t}}(t)$$

is a sequential function.
The first condition is trivially satisfied. Further we have

$$(F_1)_p(y_1(1),y_2(1))(y_1(2),y_2(2))\ldots(y_1(s),y_2(s))) = y_{\overline{l(p)+1}}(1)y_{\overline{l(p)+2}}(2)\ldots y_{\overline{l(p)+s}}(s) ,$$

and thus $|Z_{F_1}| = 2$.

Example 2.2. Again, let $X = \{0,1\}^2$, $Y = \{0,1\}$. We define F_2 by

$$F_2((x_1(1),x_2(1))(x_1(2),x_2(2))\dots(x_1(t),x_2(t)))$$

$$= \begin{cases} 1^t & \text{if } x_1(1) = 1 \\ 0^j x_2(j+1)x_2(j+2)\dots x_2(t) & \text{if } x_1(1) = x_1(2) = \dots = x_1(j) = 0 \\ & \text{and } x_1(j+1) = 1,\ j > 0 . \end{cases}$$

In this case we obtain:

if $p = (1,x_2(1))(x_1(2),x_2(2))\dots(x_1(t),x_2(t))$, then $(F_2)_p(q) = 1^{l(q)}$

if $p = (0,x_2(1))(0,x_2(2))\dots(0,x_2(j))(1,x_2(j+1))(x_1(j+2),x_2(j+2))\dots$
$\dots(x_1(t),x_2(t))$,

then $(F_2)_p((y_1(1),y_2(1))\dots(y_1(s),y_2(s))) = y_2(1)y_2(2)\dots y_2(s)$,

if $p = (0,x_2(1))(0,x_2(2))\dots(0,x_2(t))$, then

$(F_2)_p((y_1(1),y_2(1))\dots(y_1(s),y_2(s))) = 0^r y_2(r+1)y_2(r+2)\dots y_2(s)$,

where $y_1(1) = y_1(2) = \dots = y_1(r) = 0$, $y_1(r+1) = 1$.

Hence we conclude that $|Z_{F_2}| = 4$.

Example 2.3. Consider the function $F_3 : \{0,1\}^* \to \{0,1\}^*$ given by

$$F_3(p) = a_1a_2\dots a_{l(p)}$$

where

$$a_i = \begin{cases} 0 & \text{if } i \text{ is not a prime number} \\ 1 & \text{otherwise} \end{cases} \qquad \text{for } i \geq 1.$$

Obviously, $F_3(p)$ depends only on the length of p and

$$(F_3)_p = (F_3)_q \quad \text{if} \quad l(p) = l(q).$$

We prove that F_3 is not a sequential function. Suppose the contrary. Then Z_{F_3} is finite. Since the set of prime numbers is infinite, there exists a minimal number t such that, if $l(q) \geq t$ and

$$(F_3)_p(q) = b_1b_2\dots b_{l(q)},$$

then $b_j = 1$ for some $j \leq t$. Now consider the first t prime numbers $p_1p_2,\dots,p_t$ and $n = p_1p_2\dots p_t + 1$. Let p' be a word of length n. Then

$$(F_3)_{p'}(q) = 0^{p_t}b_{p_t+1}b_{p_t+2}\dots b_{l(q)}$$

for q with $l(q) \geq n$. Since $p_t > t$, this contradicts the above assertion.

We notice two properties of sequential functions. We have

$$F(pqr) = F(pq)F_{pq}(r) = F(p)F_p(q)F_{pq}(r)$$

and

$$F(pqr) = F(p)F_p(qr).$$

Therefore

$$F_p(qr) = F_p(q)F_{pq}(r),$$

and this implies that, for every $p \in X^*$, F_p is sequential, too. Further

$$F_p = F_q \quad \text{implies} \quad F_{pr} = F_{qr} \quad \text{for all} \quad r \in X^*$$

because

$$F_p(rr') = F_p(r)F_{pr}(r') \quad \text{and} \quad F_q(rr') = F_q(r)F_{qr}(r').$$

Our second approach is based on automata. In the literature there are a lot of concepts of an automaton in order to model real automata of several types. In this monograph we shall only use one of the most general abstract automata: the finite initial deterministic Mealy automaton with outputs. We recall briefly those definitions and statements which are of interest for our purposes. For further information we refer to /St/ and /GP/.

An automaton $\mathfrak{A}$ is a 6-tuple $\mathfrak{A} = (X, Y, Z, g, f, z_0)$ where

i) X, Y, Z are finite, nonempty sets,

ii) g is a function from $Z \times X$ in Z,

iii) f is a function from $Z \times X$ in Y,

iv) $z_0 \in Z$.

As usual we say that X is the input alphabet, Y is the output alphabet, Z is the set of states, g is the transition function which determines the next state if a state and an input signal are given, f is the output function, z_0 is the initial state. First we extend the functions g and f such that they are defined on $Z \times X^*$. We put

$$g(z, \lambda) = z, \qquad g(z,px) = g(g(z,p),x),$$
$$f(z, \lambda) = \lambda, \qquad f(z,px) = f(g(z,p),x).$$

(More precisely, we have to use new symbols for the extensions of g and f, but in order to simplify the notation we shall use the same symbols.)Now we can define a function which describes the input-output-behaviour of the automaton.

The induced function $F_{\mathfrak{A}}$ of the automaton $\mathfrak{A} = (X, Y, Z, g, f, z_o)$ is given by

$$F_{\mathfrak{A}}(x_1x_2\ldots x_n) = f(z_o,x_1)f(z_o,x_1x_2)\ldots f(z_o,x_1x_2\ldots x_n).$$

Example 2.4. We consider the automaton

$$\mathfrak{A}_1 = (\{0,1\}^2, \{0,1\}, \{z_o,z_1\}, g_1, f_1, z_o)$$

where the functions g_1 and f_1 are given by the following tables (the values $g_1(z,x)$ and $f_1(z,x)$ are shown in the intersection of the row and column which correspond to x and z, respectively).

g_1	z_o	z_1
(0,0)	z_1	z_o
(0,1)	z_1	z_o
(1.0)	z_1	z_o
(1,1)	z_1	z_o

f_1	z_o	z_1
(0,0)	0	0
(0,1)	0	1
(1,0)	1	0
(1,1)	1	1

Obviously, for $p \in (\{0,1\}^2)^*$,

$$g_1(z_o,p) = z_{l(p) \bmod 2} ,$$

$$f_1(z_o,p) = \begin{cases} x & \text{if } l(p) \text{ is even} \\ y & \text{if } l(p) \text{ is odd} \end{cases} ,$$

where the $l(p)$-th letter of p is (x,y), and thus

$$F_{\mathfrak{A}_1}((x_1,y_1)(x_2,y_2)\ldots(x_r,y_r)) = \begin{cases} x_1y_2x_3\ldots x_{r-1}y_r & \text{if } r \text{ is even} \\ x_1y_2x_3\ldots y_{r-1}x_r & \text{if } r \text{ is odd,} \end{cases}$$

i.e. $F_{\mathfrak{A}_1} = F_1$ (see Example 2.1.)

The latter equation will be generalized by the following two lemmas.

| Lemma 2.1. The induced function of an automaton is sequential.

Proof. Let $\mathfrak{A} = (X, Y, Z, g, f, z_o)$, $p = x_1x_2...x_n$, $r = y_1y_2...y_m$. Since

$$F_{\mathfrak{A}}(pr) = f(z_o,x_1)f(z_o,x_1x_2)...f(z_o,x_1x_2...x_n)\cdot f(z_o,x_1x_2...x_ny_1)...f(z_o,x_1x_2...x_ny_1y_2...y_m)$$

$$= F_{\mathfrak{A}}(p)f(g(z_o,p),y_1)f(g(z_o,p),y_1y_2)...f(g(z_o,p),y_1...y_m)$$

we have

$$(F_{\mathfrak{A}})_p(r) = f(g(z_o,p),y_1)f(g(z_o,p),y_1y_2)...f(g(z_o,p),y_1y_2...y_m).$$

Further, if $g(z_o,p) = g(z_o,q)$, then $(F_{\mathfrak{A}})_p = (F_{\mathfrak{A}})_q$. Because the number of states of $\mathfrak{A}$ is finite, we conclude that $Z_{F_{\mathfrak{A}}}$ is finite.

Lemma 2.2. For every sequential function F, there exists an automaton $\mathfrak{A}$ such that $F = F_{\mathfrak{A}}$.

Proof. With the sequential function F we associate the automaton

$$\mathfrak{A}_F = (X, Y, Z_F, f, g, F)$$

where

$$g(F_p,x) = F_{px} \quad \text{and} \quad f(F_p,x) = F_p(x).$$

(By the remark after Example 2.3., this definition is correct since it is independent of the used representant.) By induction, it is easy to prove that

$$g(F_p,q) = F_{pq} \quad \text{and} \quad f(F_p,qr) = F_{pq}(r).$$

Therefore we obtain

$$F_{(\mathfrak{A}_F)}(x_1x_2...x_n) = f(F_\lambda,x_1)f(F_\lambda,x_1x_2)...f(F_\lambda,x_1x_2...x_n)$$
$$= F(x_1)F_{x_1}(x_2)F_{x_1x_2}(x_3)...F_{x_1x_2...x_{n-1}}(x_n)$$
$$= F(x_1x_2)F_{x_1x_2}(x_3)...F_{x_1x_2...x_{n-1}}(x_n)$$
$$......$$
$$= F(x_1x_2...x_n).$$

The third concept is the logical net which we shall define by graph-theoretical means. A finite directed graph is a pair $G = (E, K)$ where E is a finite nonempty set and K is a subset of $E \times E$. The elements of E and K are called nodes and edges, respectively. We use graphs with labelled nodes, and hence we write the nodes as a pair (e,l) where e is the name of the node and l is its label. A path from e to e' is a sequence $k_1, k_2, \ldots, k_r$ of edges such that

$$k_i = (e_i, e_{i+1}), \quad e_1 = e, \quad e_{r+1} = e'.$$

$e_1, e_2, \ldots, e_{r+1}$ are the nodes of the path. For a node e of the graph (E, K), we put

$$i(e) = \{e' : e' \in E, (e',e) \in K\}$$

and

$$o(e) = \{e' : e' \in E, (e,e') \in K\}.$$

Now we define inductively a special class of finite graphs with labels in the set

$$\{\text{min}, \text{max}, \text{cyc}, S, i, o\},$$

the so-called logical nets, by the following conditions:

1° The graphs

$$G_1 = (\{(1,i), (2,i), (3,\text{min}), (4,o)\}, \{(1,3), (2,3), (3,4)\}),$$

$$G_2 = (\{(1,i), (2,i), (3,\text{max}), (4,o)\}, \{(1,3), (2,3), (3,4)\}),$$

$$G_3 = (\{(1,i), (2,\text{cyc}), (3,o)\}, \{(1,2), (2,3)\}),$$

$$G_4 = (\{(1,i), (2,S), (3,o)\}, \{(1,2), (2,3)\})$$

are logical nets.

Let $G = (E, K)$ and $G' = (E', K')$ be logical nets such that $E \cap E' = \emptyset$. Let e_1, e_2, e_3 be distinct nodes of G labelled by i, i, o, respectively, and let e_4 be a node of G' labelled by i. Then

2° $(E \cup E', K \cup K')$ is a logical net,

3° $(E \setminus \{e_2\}, (K \cup (\{e_1\} \times o(e_2))) \setminus (\{e_2\} \times o(e_2)))$ is a logical net,

4° the graph with the node set $(E \setminus \{e_3\}) \cup (E' \setminus \{e_4\})$ and the edge set $(K \cup K' \cup (i(e_3) \times o(e_4))) \setminus ((i(e_3) \times \{e_3\}) \cup (\{e_4\} \times o(e_4)))$ is a logical net,

5° $(E \setminus \{e_1\}, (K \setminus (\{e_1\} \times o(e_1))) \cup (i(e_3) \times o(e_1)))$ is a logical net iff any path from e_1 to e_3 contains at most one node labelled by S.

Figure 1 illustrates the definition of 3°, 4°, and 5°.

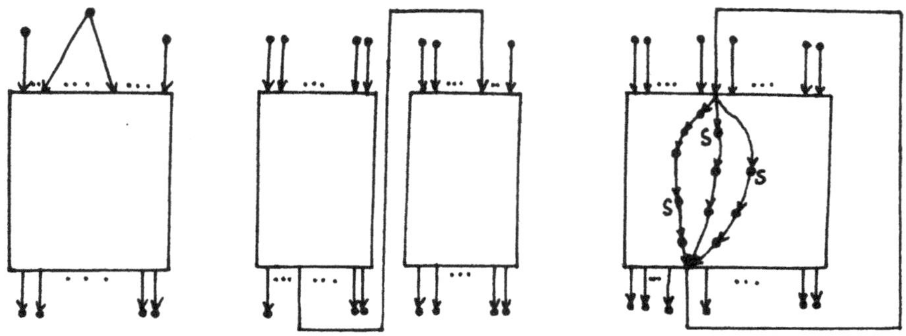

Figure 1

In order to define the functioning of a logical net we have to describe only the functioning of the elementary nets G_1, G_2, G_3, G_4 since the complete behaviour follows from the inductive constructions. We interprete the nodes labelled by i as input lines or sources which emit the signal $x(t)$ at the time moment t (we assume that $t \in \mathbb{N}$). Without loss of generality we suppose that the signals are from the set $E_k = \{0,1,\dots,k-1\}$, $k \geq 2$. The nodes labelled by o correspond to output lines which accept the reaction of the net. The nodes labelled by min, max, cyc, and S are interpreted as gates realizing certain functions or a store. If a node with label min or max receives the signals $x_1(t)$ and $x_2(t)$ at the time moment t, then it emits the minimum or the maximum of these two signals at the same time moment. If the node is labelled by cyc, its reaction on the receiving signal $x(t)$ at the moment t is $x(t) + 1 \bmod k$. If the label is S, then the gate stores the incoming signal $x(t)$ during one time moment and emits it at the time moment $t + 1$. To complete the definition we put that the emitted signal of a node labelled by S is 0 at the first moment.

Now, for any time moment t and any output line of a logical net we can determine the output $y(t)$ at the time moment t. The calculation of the value $y(t)$ can be done in the following way. We consider the last node of the net which is before the node labelled by o. If it is labelled by min, max, or cyc, we have

$$y(t) = \min(x_1(t), x_2(t)) \quad \text{or} \quad y(t) = \max(x_1(t), x_2(t))$$

$$\text{and } y(t) = \mathrm{cyc}(x(t)) = x(t) + 1 \bmod k,$$

respectively, where $x_1(t)$, $x_2(t)$, $x(t)$ are the input signals receiving the node at the time moment t. If the label is S, then the output is the signal which receives the node at the moment t-1 and it is stored. This can be described by

$$y(t) = x(t-1)$$

or, if we denote the stored signal by $q(t)$, we have

$$y(t) = q(t-1) \quad \text{and} \quad q(t-1) = x(t-1).$$

Now the inputs of the last node can be regarded as the outputs of the subgraph which contains only the nodes and edges preceding this node. Again, we determine the new outputs as above, and then we can substitute the result for $x_1(t)$, $x_2(t)$, $x(t)$, and $q(t-1)$. The process is finished if we obtain a function

$$(*) \quad y(t) = f(x_1(t),x_2(t),\ldots,x_n(t),q_1(t-1),q_2(t-1),\ldots,q_r(t-1))$$

where $x_1(t),x_2(t),\ldots,x_n(t)$ are the input signals emitted by the nodes with label i at the time moment t, and $q_1(t),q_2(t),\ldots,q_r(t)$ are the signals stored by the elements labelled by S at the time moment t. Indeed, $y(t)$ essentially depends only on the nodes with label i and S from which there is a path to the output line which contains no element labelled by S. In the same way we obtain functions to calculate the values $q_1(t),q_2(t),\ldots,q_r(t)$, i.e.

$$(**) \quad q_i(t) = g_i(x_1(t),x_2(t),\ldots,x_n(t),q_1(t-1),q_2(t-1),\ldots,q_r(t-1)).$$

The values $q_i(0)$ which are needed are 0. The equations (*) and (**) form the canonical system of equations of the net.

Let N be a logical net with n input lines and m output nodes. Then we have an input vector $(x_1(t),x_2(t),\ldots,x_n(t))$ and an output vector $(y_1(t),y_2(t),\ldots,y_m(t))$ at the time moment t. The induced function F_N of N is defined by

$$F_N(\lambda) = \lambda,$$

$$F_N((x_1(1),x_2(1),\ldots,x_n(1))\ldots(x_1(t),x_2(t),\ldots,x_n(t)))$$
$$= (y_1(1),y_2(1),\ldots,y_m(1))\ldots(y_1(t),y_2(t),\ldots,y_m(t)).$$

Using the above interpretation of a net the constructions 3°, 4°, and 5° correspond to the identification of two sources (i.e. they emit the same signals), the substitution of a source by the output of another net, and the feedback, respectively.

__Example 2.5.__ Let $k = 2$. Consider the net of Figure 2.

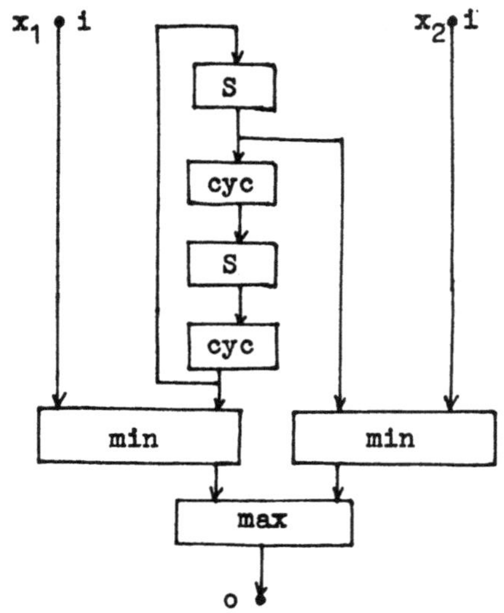

Figure 2

We obtain the following canonical system of equations

$$y(t) = \max(\min(x_1(t), \operatorname{cyc}(q_2(t-1))), \min(q_1(t-1), x_2(t))),$$

$$q_1(t) = \operatorname{cyc}(q_2(t-1)),$$

$$q_2(t) = \operatorname{cyc}(q_1(t-1)).$$

Therefore the sequences of stored signals are given by

$$q_i(t) = \begin{cases} 0 & \text{iff } t \text{ is even} \\ 1 & \text{iff } t \text{ is odd} \end{cases}, \quad i = 1,2,$$

and we have

$$y(t) = \begin{cases} x_1(t) & \text{if } t \text{ is odd} \\ x_2(t) & \text{if } t \text{ is even.} \end{cases}$$

We conclude that

$$F_N = F_1 = F_{\mathfrak{a}_1}$$

where F_1 and $F_{\mathfrak{a}_1}$ are given in the examples 2.1. and 2.4..

Lemma 2.3. For every logical net N, there exists an automaton $\mathfrak{A}$ such that $F_N = F_{\mathfrak{A}}$.

Proof. Let N be a net with n input nodes, m output nodes, and r nodes with label S. Then the functioning of N can be described by the equations

$$y_1(t) = f_1(x_1(t),x_2(t),\ldots,x_n(t),q_1(t-1),q_2(t-1),\ldots,q_r(t-1)),$$

$$\cdots\cdot$$

$$y_m(t) = f_m(x_1(t),x_2(t),\ldots,x_n(t),q_1(t-1),q_2(t-1),\ldots,q_r(t-1)),$$

$$q_1(t) = g_1(x_1(t),x_2(t),\ldots,x_n(t),q_1(t-1),q_2(t-1),\ldots,q_r(t-1)),$$

$$\cdots\cdot$$

$$q_r(t) = g_r(x_1(t),x_2(t),\ldots,x_n(t),q_1(t-1),q_2(t-1),\ldots,q_r(t-1)).$$

We consider the automaton

$$\mathfrak{A} = (E_k{}^n,\ E_k{}^m,\ E_k{}^r,\ g,\ f,\ (0,0,\ldots,0)\ )$$

with

$$g((z_1,z_2,\ldots,z_r),(x_1,x_2,\ldots,x_n))$$
$$= (g_1(x_1,\ldots,x_n,z_1,\ldots,z_r),\ldots,g_r(x_1,\ldots,x_n,z_1,\ldots,z_r)),$$

$$f((z_1,z_2,\ldots,z_r),(x_1,x_2,\ldots,x_n))$$
$$= (f_1(x_1,\ldots,x_n,z_1,\ldots,z_r),\ldots,f_m(x_1,\ldots,x_n,z_1,\ldots,z_r)).$$

Indeed, $F_N = F_{\mathfrak{A}}$.

Lemma 2.4. If the input and output alphabet of the automaton $\mathfrak{A}$ are cartesian powers of E_k, then there exists a logical net N such that $F_N = F_{\mathfrak{A}}$.

Proof. Let $\mathfrak{A} = (E_k{}^n,\ E_k{}^m,\ Z,\ g,\ f,\ z_o)$ and $|Z| = u$. Then there exists a natural number r such that $k^{r-1} < u \leq k^r$. Therefore we can define a bijective function ς from Z in $E_k{}^r$ such that

$$\varsigma(z_o) = (0,0,\ldots,0).$$

Let

$$\mathfrak{A}' = (E_k{}^n,\ E_k{}^m,\ E_k{}^r,\ g',\ f',\ (0,0,\ldots,0)\ )$$

where

$$g'(z,x) = \begin{cases} \varrho(g(\varrho^{-1}(z),x)) & \text{if } \varrho^{-1}(z) \text{ exists} \\ (0,0,\dots,0) & \text{otherwise,} \end{cases}$$

$$f'(z,x) = \begin{cases} f(\varrho^{-1}(z),x) & \text{if } \varrho^{-1}(z) \text{ exists} \\ (0,0,\dots,0) & \text{otherwise.} \end{cases}$$

Evidently, $F_{\mathfrak{A}} = F_{\mathfrak{A}'}$. We can split the functions g' and f' in the following way:

$$g'((z_1,z_2,\dots,z_r),(x_1,x_2,\dots,x_n))$$
$$=(g_1(z_1,\dots,z_r,x_1,\dots,x_n),\dots,g_r(z_1,\dots,z_r,x_1,\dots,x_n)),$$

$$f'((z_1,z_2,\dots,z_r),(x_1,x_2,\dots,x_n))$$
$$=(f_1(z_1,\dots,z_r,x_1,\dots,x_n),\dots,f_m(z_1,\dots,z_r,x_1,\dots,x_n)).$$

We now prove that, for any function $h : E_k{}^s \rightarrow E_k$, there exists a logical net such that

$$y(t) = h(x_1(t),x_2(t),\dots,x_s(t)).$$

Let σ be the function defined by

$$\sigma(x) = \begin{cases} 0 & \text{if } x = \sigma \\ k-1 & \text{if } x \neq \sigma \end{cases},$$

and, for $0 \leq i \leq k-1$, let k_i be the constant function given by

$$k_i(x) = i \;,$$

Since

$$\sigma(x) = \text{cyc}^{k-1}(\min(\text{cyc}^{1-\sigma}(x),\text{cyc}^{2-\sigma}(x),\dots,\text{cyc}^{k-1-\sigma}(x))),$$

(inductively we define $\min(x_1,x_2,\dots,x_n)=\min(\min(x_1,x_2,\dots,x_{n-1}),x_n))$

$$k_i(x) = \text{cyc}^i(\min(x,\text{cyc}(x),\text{cyc}^2(x),\dots,\ \text{cyc}^{k-1}(x))),$$

$$h(x_1,x_2,\dots,x_s)$$
$$= \min_{(\sigma_1,\dots,\sigma_s)\in E_k{}^s} \max(h(\sigma_1,\sigma_2,\dots,\sigma_s),\sigma_1(x_1),\sigma_2(x_2),\dots,\sigma_n(x_n))$$

and the construction 4^0 models the substitution of functions, the existence of such a logical net is shown.
Then the net of Figure 3 satisfies $F_N = F_{\mathfrak{A}'} = F_{\mathfrak{A}}$.

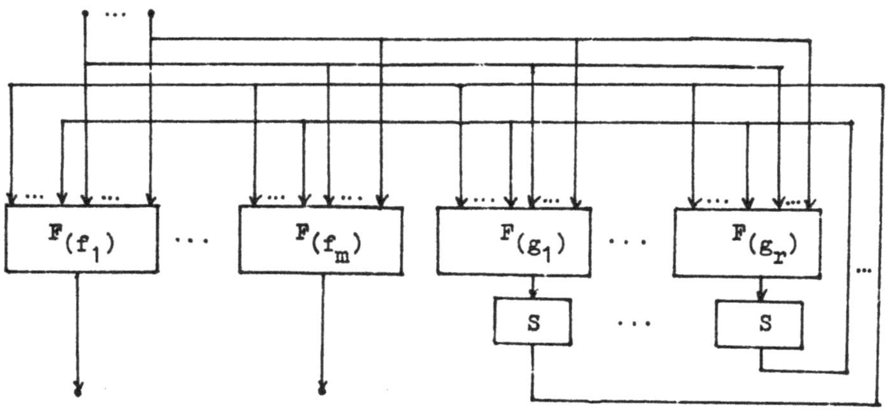

Figure 3. The node $F_{(u)}$ represents a graph corresponding to a net with the output function $y(t) = u(x_1(t), x_2(t), \dots, x_{n+r}(t))$.

Summarizing our lemmas we have

<u>Theorem 2.5.</u> Let $F : (E_k{}^n)^* \to (E_k{}^m)^*$ be a function. Then the following statements are equivalent:

i) F is a sequential function.
ii) F is induced by an automaton.
iii) F is induced by a logical net.

Let $F : (E_k{}^n)^* \to (E_k{}^m)^*$ be a sequential function and

$$F((x_1(1),\dots,x_n(1))\dots(x_1(t),\dots,x_n(t))) \\ =(y_1(1),\dots,y_m(1))\dots(y_1(t),\dots,y_m(t)).$$

Then we can split it componentwise, i.e.

$$F = (F_1, F_2, \dots, F_m)$$

where, for $i = 1,2,\dots,m$,

$$F_i((x_1(1),\dots,x_n(1)),\dots,(x_1(t),\dots,x_n(t)) = y_i(1)\dots y_i(t).$$

Therefore the set of sequential functions $F : (E_k{}^n)^* \to E_k{}^*$ is of special interest. We put

$$P_k{}^n = \{F : F : (E_k{}^n)^* \to E_k{}^*\}$$

(as usual in universal algebra $P_k{}^0$ is the set of constant mappings) and

$$P_k = \bigcup_{n \geq 0} P_k{}^n .$$

Since we are interested in the input-output-behaviour which can be induced by automata or logical nets, the special structure of the automaton or logical net is of no importance. Therefore P_k will be the underlying set of our algebra.

Lemma 2.6. The cardinality of P_k is $\aleph_0$.

Proof. Because two automata can induce the same sequential function, we obtain that the cardinality of P_k is smaller than that of the set $\bigcup_{i\geq 1} \bigcup_{j\geq 1} \mathfrak{A}_i^j$, where $\mathfrak{A}_i^j$ is the set of all automata with the input alphabet $E_k{}^i$, output alphabet E_k, and a set Z of states with $|Z| = j$ (observe that the notation of the elements of Z is not important). Since $\mathfrak{A}_i^j$ is a finite set, we have $|P_k| \leq \aleph_0$.
Conversely, P_k contains the elements F_j, $j \in \mathbb{N}$, defined by

$$F_j(p) = \begin{cases} 0 & \text{if } l(p) = j \\ 1 & \text{otherwise.} \end{cases}$$

This implies $|P_k| \geq \aleph_0$.

Finally we introduce some notations for sequential functions in P_k. We can see from the definition of the functions induced by automata or logical nets that we can describe a sequential function $F : X^* \longrightarrow Y^*$ by an infinite sequence

$$(\varphi_F^1, \varphi_F^2, \ldots, \varphi_F^t, \ldots)$$

where φ_F^t is a function which maps X^t in Y such that

$$F(a_1 a_2 \ldots a_n) = \varphi_F^1(a_1)\,\varphi_F^2(a_1,a_2) \ldots \varphi_F^n(a_1,a_2,\ldots,a_n),$$

i.e. φ_F^t determines the t-th letter of $F(p)$ and depends on the first t letters of p. (Observe that other functions can also be described in this way, for instance F_3 of Example 2.3..)
A function $F \in P_k$ is defined over $(E_k{}^n)^*$ for some n, i.e. its domain consists of words

$$p = (x_1(1),\ldots,x_n(1))(x_1(2),\ldots,x_n(2))\ldots(x_1(t),\ldots,x_n(t)).$$

If we regard F as a function induced by a logical net, the i-th input line emits the word $x_i(1)x_i(2)\ldots x_i(t)$. Therefore we split p and write

$$p = (p_1, p_2, \ldots, p_n)$$

where

$$p_i = x_i(1)x_i(2)\dots x_i(t).$$

Instead of $F((p_1,p_2,\dots,p_n))$ we shall only write $F(p_1,p_2,\dots,p_n)$. This notation will be useful in the next paragraph if we introduce the operations of the algebra which are based on the constructions of logical nets. Further, we can regard the elements of $P_k{}^n$ as partial functions on $(E_k{}^*)^n$, where the partiality arises from the requirement that the words p_i, $1 \le i \le n$, have to have the same length. In the following chapters sequential functions will be often defined only by the direct description of $F(p)$ or by the sequence $(\varphi_F^1, \varphi_F^2, \dots)$, and the complete proof that the function is sequential will be omitted and left to the reader.

Sometimes we need an extension of sequential functions on ω-words. We put

$$F(a_1a_2\dots) = y_1y_2\dots$$

where

$$y_i = \varphi_F^i(a_1,a_2,\dots,a_i).$$

Lemma 2.7. Let $F : X^* \longrightarrow Y^*$ be a sequential function of weight n, and let α be a periodic ω-word over X with period s. Then $F(\alpha)$ is a periodic ω-word with period r where $r = k \cdot s$ for some $k \le n$.

Proof. Let $\mathfrak{A} = (X, Y, Z, g, f, z_o)$ be an automaton such that $F_{\mathfrak{A}} = F$. Further let $\alpha = a_1a_2\dots$ and $a_i = a_{i+s}$ for $i > t$. We put

$$z_j = g(z_o, a_1a_2\dots a_j)$$

and consider the states $z_t, z_{t+s}, z_{t+2s},\dots,tz_{t+ns}$. Since $\mathfrak{A}$ has only n states, two of these states coincide. Let

$$z_{t+is} = z_{t+js} \quad \text{for} \quad 0 \le i < j \le n.$$

Then we have

$$z_{t+is+k} = z_{t+js+k} \quad \text{for} \quad k \ge 0$$

by the periodicity of α, and further,

$$\begin{aligned} y_{t+is+k+1} &= f(z_{t+is+k}, a_{t+is+k+1}) \\ &= f(z_{t+js+k}, a_{t+js+k+1}) \\ &= y_{t+js+k+1}. \end{aligned}$$

2.2. Composition of Sequential Functions

In this paragraph we introduce the operations of our algebra. To do this we shall translate the principles of constructions of logical nets to sequential functions.

Let $F \in P_k^n$, $n \geq 2$. Then we put

$$(\zeta F)(p_1,p_2,\dots,p_n) = F(p_2,p_3,\dots,p_n,p_1),$$

$$(\tau F)(p_1,p_2,\dots,p_n) = F(p_2,p_1,p_3,p_4,\dots,p_n),$$

$$(\Delta F)(p_1,p_2,\dots,p_{n-1}) = F(p_1,p_1,p_2,p_3,\dots,p_{n-1}).$$

If $F \in P_k^n$, $n \leq 1$, then we define $\zeta F = \tau F = \Delta F = F$.

Let $F \in P_k^n$, $G \in P_k^m$, $n \geq 1$, $m \geq 0$, then we put

$$(F \circ G)(p_1,p_2,\dots,p_{n+m-1}) = F(G(p_1,p_2,\dots,p_m),p_{m+1},p_{m+2},\dots,p_{n+m-1})$$

If $F \in P_k^0$, then $F \circ G = F$.

The operations ζ and τ are of technical nature and correspond to special permutations of the input lines or variables. It is well-known that the associated permutations form a basis of the group of permutations of n elements and therefore we can generate any permutation of the variables as a new operation if we apply ζ and τ sometimes. The operations Δ and $\circ$ describe the identification of special input lines and the substitution for the first variable. If we combine these operations with certain permutations of variables, we can generate the operations: identification of arbitrary variables (also more than two variables if we sometimes use Δ) and the substitution at any place and an arbitrary number of substitutions, etc.
We say that the i-th variable of $F \in P_k$ is essential iff there exist words $p_1,p_2,\dots,p_n \in E_k^*$, $q_i \in E_k^*$ such that

$$F(p_1,p_2,\dots,p_i,\dots,p_n) \neq F(p_1,p_2,\dots,p_{i-1},q_i,p_{i+1},p_{i+2},\dots,p_n).$$

A variable which is not essential is called a dummy variable. If the i-th variable of F is dummy, then the value of F does not depend on the words which the i-th source emits. Therefore it is often customary to identify sequential functions which differ only in the number and/or order of dummy variables. We shall use another equivalent approach. Applying ζ and τ we can permute the dummy variables. Further we can generate the elimination of dummy variables by applications of Δ, ζ, and τ. For instance, if the first variable of F is dummy, then the function which is obtained by omitting the (first) dummy variable coincides with ΔF. We introduce the adding of a dummy variable as a new operation: If $F \in P_k{}^n$, $n \geq 0$, then $\nabla F \in P_k{}^{n+1}$ is given by

$$(\nabla F)(p_1, p_2, \dots, p_{n+1}) = F(p_1, p_2, \dots, p_n).$$

Therefore we can generate from $F \in P_k$ all functions $F' \in P_k$ which differ from F in the number and/or order of dummy variables.
Let $F \in P_k{}^n$, and let $(\varphi_F^1, \varphi_F^2, \dots)$ be its description by an infinite sequence of functions $\varphi_F^i : E_k{}^{ni} \to E_k$. We say that F depends delayed on the first variable if, for every $t \geq 1$, the function φ_F^t does not depend on $x_1(t)$ essentially (the essential dependence is defined in an analogous way as for sequential functions).
Now let $F \in P_k{}^n$, $n \geq 1$, depend delayed on its first variable. Then the feedback of F is defined as $\times F \in P_k{}^{n-1}$, which is given by the functions

$$\varphi_{\times F}^1(x_2(1), x_3(1), \dots, x_n(1)) = \varphi_F^1(x_1(1), x_2(1), \dots, x_n(1)),$$

$$\begin{aligned} \varphi_{\times F}^t(x_2(1), \dots, x_n(1), x_2(2), \dots, x_n(2), \dots, x_2(t), \dots, x_n(t)) \\ = \varphi_F^t(\varphi_{\times F}^1(z_1), x_2(1), \dots, x_n(1), \\ \varphi_{\times F}^2(z_2), x_2(2), \dots, x_n(2), \dots \\ \varphi_{\times F}^{t-1}(z_{t-1}), x_2(t-1), \dots, x_n(t-1), \\ x_2(t), \dots, x_n(t)) \quad \text{for } t \geq 2 \end{aligned}$$ [1],

where z_i is the tupel of the variables of φ_F^i.
We remark that the feedback $\times$ is a partial operation. Obviously, if the first variable of the sequential function F is dummy, then F depends delayed on the first variable and we can apply the feeback operation and obtain $\Delta F = \times F$. Thus the feedback is only of interest if the first variable is not a dummy variable. Therefore we shall say in the sequel that the operation $\times$ is not applicable if F does not depend delayed on its essential variables.
By the above definition, we have immediately

<u>Lemma 2.8.</u> If $G = \times F$, then $F \circ G = G$.

---

[1] For simplicity, we write
$\varphi_F^t(x_1(1), \dots, x_n(1), x_1(2), \dots, x_n(2), \dots, x_1(t), \dots, x_n(t))$ instead of
$\varphi_F^t((x_1(1), \dots, x_n(1)), (x_1(2), \dots, x_n(2)), \dots, (x_1(t), \dots, x_n(t)))$

Furthermore, the application of one of the above operations to sequential functions leads to sequential functions. This is obvious with respect to ζ, τ, and ∇, and it follows for Δ, $\circ$, $\times$ by the fact that these operations model the constructions for logical nets.

<u>Example 2.6.</u> Consider the sequential functions $F_1 \in P_k^{\,2}$, $F_2 \in P_k^{\,2}$, and $F_3 \in P_k^{\,1}$ defined by

$$\varphi^{1}_{F_1}(x_1(1),x_2(1)) = 0,$$

$$\varphi^{t}_{F_1}(x_1(1),x_2(1),\ldots,x_1(t),x_2(t)) = \min(x_1(t-1),x_2(t)) \quad \text{for } t \geq 2,$$

$$\varphi^{1}_{F_2}(x_1(1),x_2(1)) = x_2(1),$$

$$\varphi^{t}_{F_2}(x_1(1),x_2(1),\ldots,x_1(t),x_2(t)) = \max(x_1(t),x_2(t-1)) \quad \text{for } t \geq 2,$$

$$\varphi^{1}_{F_3}(x(1)) = 0, \qquad \varphi^{2}_{F_3}(x(1),x(2)) = x(1),$$

$$\varphi^{t}_{F_3}(x(1),\ldots,x(t)) = \max(x(t-1),\min(x(t),\varphi^{t-1}_{F_3}(x(1),\ldots,x(t-1)))) \quad \text{for } t \geq 2.$$

Then $F_3 = \times\,\tau\,\Delta\,\zeta\,(F_2 \circ F_1)$. The logical nets associated with these functions are given in Figure 4. We can also describe the net F_3 by the net of Figure 5 where the nodes F_1 and F_2 stand for the corresponding subnets. We see that there are different descriptions of the constructions of F_3 from F_1 and F_2. In the sequel we shall most frequently use the description of Figure 5 which seems to be the most illustrative and simplest one.

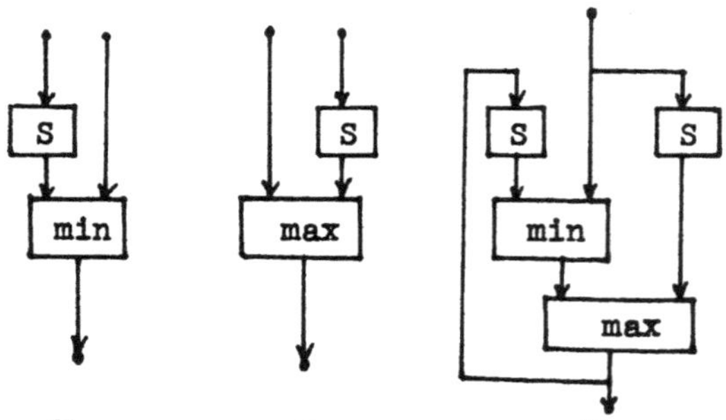

F_1 $\qquad$ F_2 $\qquad$ F_3

Figure 4

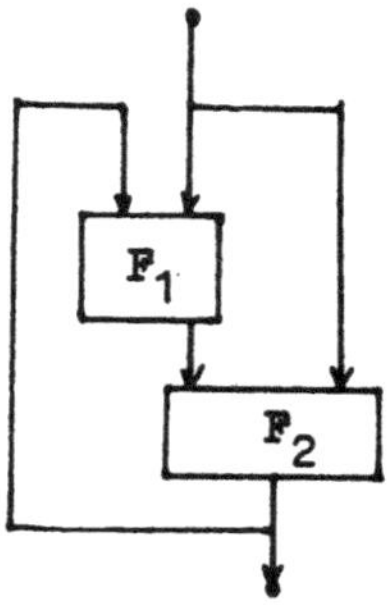

Figure 5

The subject of this monograph is the study of the algebra

$$\underline{P_k} = (P_k;\ \zeta, \tau, \Delta, \circ, \nabla, \times)$$

and its completeness problem, i.e. the question of generation of P_k by its subsets. Especially, we shall be interested in the following questions:

i) Does there exist a criterion for completeness in $\underline{P_k}$?

ii) Does there exist an algorithm to decide the completeness in $\underline{P_k}$?

Let $M \subseteq P_k$. In terms of logical nets we can interprete the completeness problem as follows: Given an arbitrary function $F \in P_k$, can we construct a logical net N such that $F = F_N$, where we consider elementary nets which induce functions of M instead of the elementary nets of the definition on page 31?

We notice, we are only interested in the question whether or not a certain sequential function can be generated by a subset of P_k. We do not want to construct the most economic logical net inducing this function where the costs are measured by the number of gates in the net or another appropriate measure.

2.3. Examples of Subalgebras of $\underline{P_k}$

In this paragraph we consider some examples of subalgebras which will be needed later.

<u>Example 2.7.</u> Let

$$P_k'^{\,n} = \{f : f : E_k^{\,n} \to E_k\}$$

and

$$P_k' = \bigcup_{n \geq 0} P_k'^{\,n} .$$

For any $f \in P_k'$, we define the sequential function $F_{(f)}$ by

$$\varphi^t_{F_{(f)}}(x_1(1),\dots,x_n(1),\dots,x_1(t),\dots,x_n(t)) = f(x_1(t),\dots,x_n(t))$$

for $t \geq 1$, i.e. $F_{(f)}$ realizes the function f at any moment and cannot store information. For $R \subseteq P_k'$, we put

$$\widetilde{R} = \{F_{(f)} : f \in R\} .$$

It is easy to see that the application of the operations $\zeta, \tau, \Delta, \nabla$, and $\circ$ to functions of $\widetilde{P_k'}$ leads to functions of $\widetilde{P_k'}$. The operation cannot be applied since $F_{(f)}$ does not depend delayed on its vari-variables. Therefore

$$\underline{\widetilde{P_k'}} = (\widetilde{P_k'}; \zeta, \tau, \Delta, \circ, \nabla, \times)$$

is a subalgebra of $\underline{P_k}$, and obviously it is isomorphic to

$$(\widetilde{P_k'}; \zeta, \tau, \Delta, \circ, \nabla).$$

The elements of P_k' correspond to the functions induced by combinational logical net, i.e. by nets which do not contain the elementary net S.

For $f \in P_k'^n$, $g \in P_k'^m$, we put

$$(\zeta f)(x_1,x_2,\ldots,x_n) = f(x_2,x_3,\ldots,x_n,x_1),$$

$$(\tau f)(x_1,x_2,\ldots,x_n) = f(x_2,x_1,x_3,x_4,\ldots,x_n),$$

$$(\Delta f)(x_1,x_2,\ldots,x_{n-1}) = f(x_1,x_1,x_2,x_3,\ldots,x_{n-1}),$$

$$(\nabla f)(x_1,x_2,\ldots,x_{n+1}) = f(x_1,x_2,\ldots,x_n),$$

$$(f \circ g)(x_1,x_2,\ldots,x_{n+m-1}) = f(g(x_1,x_2,\ldots,x_m),x_{m+1},x_{m+2},\ldots,x_{n+m-1})$$

Then we obtain

$$\alpha F_{(f)} = F_{(\alpha f)} \quad \text{for} \quad \alpha \in \{\zeta, \tau, \Delta, \nabla\}$$

and

$$F_{(f)} \circ F_{(g)} = F_{(f \circ g)},$$

and therefore we have that the following algebras are isomorphic:

$$\underline{P_k'} = (P_k'; \zeta, \tau, \Delta, \circ, \nabla) \cong (\widetilde{P_k'}; \zeta, \tau, \Delta, \circ, \nabla) = \underline{\widetilde{P_k'}} .$$

The algebra $\underline{P_k'}$ will be studied in Chapter 3.

Finally we notice that if $\underline{R}$ is a subalgebra of $\underline{P_k'}$, then $\widetilde{\underline{R}}$ is a subalgebra of $\underline{\widetilde{P_k'}}$ and therefore of $\underline{P_k}$, too.

<u>Example 2.8.</u> Let $F^{(f)}$ be the sequential function defined by

$$\varphi^1_F(f) = f, \quad \varphi^t_F(f) = k_o \quad \text{for} \quad t \geq 2.$$

Again, we cannot apply the feedback operation to these functions, and we have

$$\alpha F^{(f)} = F^{(\alpha f)} \quad \text{for} \quad \alpha \in \{\zeta, \tau, \Delta, \nabla\} \quad \text{and} \quad F^{(f)} \circ F^{(g)} = F^{(f \circ g)}$$

and

$$\underline{\widetilde{P_k'}} \cong (\{F^{(f)} : f \in P_k'\}; \zeta, \tau, \Delta, \circ, \nabla).$$

Evidently, we can use as the sequence $(\varphi^2_{F^{(f)}}, \varphi^3_{F^{(f)}}, \dots)$ any sequence which describes a constant sequential function in order to obtain an algebra isomorphic to $\underline{P_k'}$.

Example 2.9. Let R be a subset of P_k', and define M_R by

$$M_R = \{F : F \in P_k,\ \varphi^1_F \in R\}.$$

If $\underline{R}$ is a subalgebra of $\underline{P_k'}$, then $\underline{M_R}$ is a subalgebra of $\underline{P_k}$. This follows by the relations

$$\varphi^1_{\alpha F} = \alpha\varphi^1_F \quad \text{for} \quad \alpha \in \{\zeta, \tau, \Delta, \nabla\}, \quad \text{and} \quad \varphi^1_{F \circ G} = \varphi^1_F \circ \varphi^1_G,$$

and the fact that φ^1_F and $\varphi^1_{\times F}$ differ only in a dummy variable.

Example 2.10. Let M^i be the set of all sequential functions $F \in P_k$ where the functions φ^i_F essentially depend at most on the variables $x_1(i), x_2(i), \dots, x_n(i)$ (n denotes the arity of F). Let $F, G \in M^i$, $F \in P_k{}^n$, $G \in P_k{}^m$. Then

$$\begin{aligned}
&\varphi^i_{F \circ G}(x_1(1), \dots, x_{n+m-1}(1), \dots, x_1(i), \dots, x_{n+m-1}(i)) \\
&= \varphi^i_F(\varphi^1_G(x_1(1), \dots, x_m(1)), x_{m+1}(1), \dots, x_{m+n-1}(1), \\
&\qquad \varphi^2_G(x_1(1), \dots, x_m(1), x_1(2), \dots, x_m(2)), x_{m+1}(2), \dots, x_{n+m-1}(2), \\
&\qquad \varphi^i_G(x_1(1), \dots, x_m(1), \dots, x_1(i), \dots, x_m(i)), x_{m+1}(i), \dots, x_{n+m-1}(i))
\end{aligned}$$

essentially depends only on $x_{m+1}(i), x_{m+2}(i), \dots, x_{n+m-1}(i)$ and the essential variables of φ^i_G, i.e. $x_1(i), x_2(i), \dots, x_n(i)$. Thus M^i is closed under $\circ$. Analogously we can prove the closure with respect to $\zeta, \tau, \Delta, \nabla$. Considering the definition of $\times$ we see that φ^i_F and $\varphi^i_{\times F}$ have the same essential variables, and we conclude that $\times F \in M^i$. Therefore $\underline{M^i}$ forms a subalgebra of $\underline{P_k}$. (Notice: $M^1 = P_k$.)

Example 2.11. Let $C \subseteq P_k{}^0$. Then the subalgebra generated by C is

$$[C] = \{F : F = \nabla^n G \text{ for some } n \in \mathbb{N} \text{ and } G \in C\}.$$

Obviously, $[C]$ has to contain all such functions F (applications of ∇). Further, if $F_1 = \nabla^n G_1$ and $F_2 = \nabla^m G_2$, then

$$\zeta F_1 = \tau F_1 = \nabla^n G_1,$$

$$\chi F_1 = \nabla^{n-1} G_1, \qquad F_1 \circ F_2 = \nabla^{n+m-1} G_1,$$

$$\Delta F_1 = \begin{cases} \nabla^{n-1} G_1 & \text{for } n \geq 2 \\ \nabla^n G_1 & \text{for } n \leq 1. \end{cases}$$

(We see that $C \neq [C]$. This relation only holds because we do not have identified functions which differ only in their dummy variables.)

Example 2.12. Let N^t be the set of all sequential functions $F \in P_k$ such that

$$\varphi_F^t(x_1(1),\ldots,x_n(1),\ldots,x_1(t),\ldots,x_n(t))$$

$$= c_o(x_1(1),\ldots,x_n(1),\ldots,x_1(t-1),\ldots,x_n(t-1))$$

$$+ \sum_{i=1}^{n} c_i(x_1(1),\ldots,x_n(1),\ldots,x_1(t-1),\ldots,x_n(t-1))x_i(t) \bmod k.$$

Evidently, the operations ζ, τ, Δ, and ∇ preserve the linearity of the functions φ_F^t in the $x_i(t)$. Let $a_i = (x_1(i),x_2(i),\ldots,x_m(i))$. Then, for $F \in P_k{}^n$, $G \in P_k{}^m$, $F,G \in N^t$,

$$\varphi_{F \circ G}^{\,t}(x_1(1),\ldots,x_{n+m-1}(1),\ldots,x_1(t),\ldots,x_{n+m-1}(t))$$

$$= c_o' + c_1' \varphi_G^t(a_1,a_2,\ldots,a_t) + \sum_{i=m+1}^{m+n-1} c_i' x_i(t) \quad \bmod k$$

where

$$c_j' = c_j(\varphi_G^1(a_1),x_{m+1}(1),\ldots,x_{m+n-1}(1),$$

$$\varphi_G^2(a_1,a_2),x_{m+1}(2),\ldots,x_{m+n-1}(2),\ldots$$

$$\varphi_G^{t-1}(a_1,a_2,\ldots,a_{t-1}),x_{m+1}(t-1),\ldots,x_{m+n-1}(t-1))$$

$$= c_j'(x_1(1),\ldots,x_{m+n-1}(1),\ldots,x_1(t-1),\ldots,x_{m+n-1}(t-1))$$

for $j \in \{0,1,m+1,m+2,m+3,\ldots,n+m-1\}$. Since

$$\varphi_G^t(x_1(1),\ldots,x_m(1),\ldots,x_1(t),\ldots,x_m(t)) = d_o + \sum_{i=1}^{m} d_i x_i(t) \bmod k,$$

we have

$$\varphi_{F \circ G}^{\,t}(x_1(1),\ldots,x_{n+m-1}(1),\ldots,x_1(t),\ldots,x_{n+m-1}(t))$$

$$= c_o' + c_1' d_o + \sum_{i=1}^{m} c_1' d_i x_i(t) + \sum_{j=m+1}^{m+n-1} c_j' x_j(t) \quad \bmod k$$

i.e. $F \circ G \in N^t$. If the feedback operation can be applied to $F \in N^t$, then F depends delayed on the first variable. Then

$$\varphi^t_F(x_1(1),\dots,x_n(1),\dots,x_1(t),\dots,x_n(t)) = c_0 + \sum_{i=2}^{n} c_i x_i(t) \mod k$$

and

$$\varphi^t_{\times F}(x_2(1),\dots,x_n(1),\dots,x_2(t),\dots,x_n(t)) = c''_0 + \sum_{i=2}^{n} c''_i x_i(t) \mod k$$

where the constants c''_i, $i = 0,2,3,\dots,n$, can be calculated in an analogous way as in case $\circ$. Thus $\underline{N^t}$ is a subalgebra.

Example 2.13. A sequential function F is called a projection iff

$$F(p_1,p_2,\dots,p_n) = p_i \quad \text{for some } i .$$

The set of all projections forms a subalgebra. Clearly, the application of $\zeta, \tau, \Delta, \nabla$ to projections gives projections, and

$$(F\circ G)(p_1,\dots,p_{n+m-1}) = \begin{cases} p_i & \text{if } F(q_1,\dots,q_n)=q_1,\ G(p_1,\dots,p_m)=p_i \\ p_{m+i-1} & \text{if } F(q_1,\dots,q_n)=q_i,\ i\geq 2. \end{cases}$$

If F is a projection, then $[\{F\}]$ equals the set of all projections. Indeed, any projection can be generated by repeated applications of ζ, τ, and ∇ or Δ. By E we denote the set of projections.

Lemma 2.9. If M is a subalgebra which contains no projection, then $[M \cup E] = M \cup E$.

Proof. Let $F, G \in M \cup E$. Then $F \in M$ or $F \in E$ and therefore, for $\alpha \in \{\zeta, \tau, \Delta, \nabla, \times\}$, $\alpha F \in M$ or $\alpha F \in E$ (in the second case $\times$ is not applicable), and thus $M \cup E$ is closed under α. We prove $F \circ G \in M \cup E$.

Case 1. $F \in M$, $G \in E$. If $F \in P_k^{\,n}$, $G \in P_k^{\,m}$, and G depends essentially on the i-th variable, $1 \leq i \leq m$, then

$$(F\circ G)(p_1,p_2,\dots,p_{n+m-1}) = F(p_i,p_{m+1},p_{m+2},\dots,p_{m+n-1}).$$

Therefore $F \circ G$ can be obtained from F by applications of ∇, ζ, and τ.

Case 2. $F \in E$, $G \in M$. Again, let $F \in P_k^{\,n}$, $G \in P_k^{\,m}$, and let F depend essentially on the i-th variable, $1 \leq i \leq n$. If $i \neq 1$, then

$$(F\circ G)(p_1,p_2,\dots,p_{n+m-1}) = p_{m+i-1}.$$

Thus $F \circ G \in E$. If $i = 1$, then

$$(F\circ G)(p_1,p_2,\dots,p_{m+n-1}) = G(p_1,p_2,\dots,p_m).$$

and therefore $F \circ G \in M$.

Case 3. $F, G \in M$. Then $F \circ G \in M$.

Case 4. $F, G \in E$. Then $F \circ G \in E$.

Finally, we define a special type of sequential functions. Let $r \geq 1$, $a_1, a_2, \ldots, a_r \in E_k$, $f \in P_k'^n$. $F_{(f;1;a_1,a_2,\ldots,a_r)}$ denotes the sequential function F given by

$$\varphi_F^i = k_{a_i} \quad \text{for} \quad 1 \leq i \leq r,$$

$$\varphi_F^j(x_1(1),x_2(1),\ldots,x_n(1),\ldots,x_1(j),x_2(j),\ldots,x_n(j))$$
$$= f(x_1(j-r),x_2(j-r),\ldots,x_n(j-r)) \quad \text{for} \quad j > r.$$

The function $F_{(id;1;0)}$, where id denotes the identity mapping on E_k, is induced by the elementary net with label S.

Exercises

1. Give an automaton and a logical net which induce the sequential function F_2 (Example2.2.).
2. Show that the function induced by the net presented in the following figure can be obtained from F_1, F_2, and F_3 by the operations of the algebra $\underline{P_k}$.

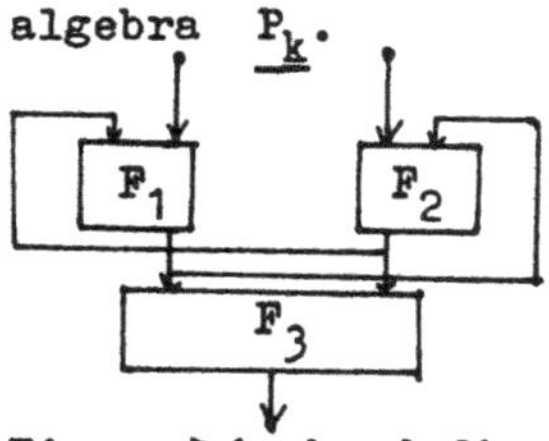

3. Let F_r and F_r', $r \geq 1$, be defined by

$$\varphi_{F_r}^t(x(1),x(2),\ldots,x(t)) = \begin{cases} x(1) & \text{if} \quad t = 2 \\ x(t) & \text{if} \quad 3 \leq t \leq r \\ 0 & \text{otherwise,} \end{cases}$$

$$\varphi_{F_r'}^t(x(1),x(2),\ldots,x(t)) = \begin{cases} x(t-1) & \text{for} \quad 2 \leq t \leq r \\ 0 & \text{otherwise.} \end{cases}$$

   a) Prove: F_r and F_r' are sequential functions.
   b) Give automata and logical nets which induce F_r or F_r'.
   c) Determine $[\{F_r\}]$ and $[\{F_r'\}]$.
4. Determine $[\{F_{(id;1;0)}\}]$.

5. Discuss whether or not the following subsets of P_k form a subalgebra of $\underline{P_k}$.

a) $S_o = \{F_{(f;s;0,0,\ldots,0)} : s \geq 1,\ f \in P_k'\}$,

b) $S_1^r = \{F_{(f;r;a_1,a_2,\ldots,a_r)} : a_i \in E_k,\ f \in P_k'\}$,

c) $S_2^r = \{F : \varphi_F^t = k_o \text{ for } t \leq r\}$,

d) $S_3^r = \{F : \varphi_F^t = k_o \text{ for } t \geq r\}$.

3. FUNCTIONS OVER A FINITE SET

In the last time some monographs and survey papers on the algebra

$$\underline{P_k'} = (P_k'; \zeta, \tau, \Delta, \nabla, \circ)$$

have been published (/Pö/, /Ro3/, /JL/, /We/). Therefore we shall give only a review, and we omit the proofs if their ideas or concepts are not used later.

Theorem 3.1. $\underline{P_k'}$ is finitely generated. Moreover, it is generated by a single function.

Proof. $P_k' = [\{cyc, min, max\}]$ is already shown in Chapter 2. We consider the function $sh \in P_k'^2$ defined by

$$sh(x,y) = min(x,y) + 1 \mod k.$$

Then

$$cyc\ (x) = sh(x,x),$$

$$min(x,y) = cyc^{k-1}(sh(x,y)).$$

By the proof of Lemma 2.4., $k_i \in [\{cyc, min\}]$ for $0 \le i \le k-1$. We define the functions $u_i \in P_k'^1$, $f_{s,i} \in P_k'^1$, $d \in P_k'^1$, $0 \le i \le k-1$, $0 \le s \le k-1$, by

$$u_i(x) = \begin{cases} k-1 & \text{if } x = i \\ 0 & \text{otherwise,} \end{cases}$$

$$f_{s,i}(x) = \begin{cases} s & \text{if } x = i \\ k-1 & \text{otherwise,} \end{cases}$$

$$d(x) = k-1 - x \mod k .$$

Then

$$u_i(x) = cyc^{k-1}(min(k_1(x), cyc^{k-1}(x))),$$

$$f_{s,i}(x) = cyc^{k-1}(min(u_i(x), k_{s+1}(x))),$$

$$d(x) = min(f_{k-1,o}(x), f_{k-2,1}(x), \ldots, f_{o,k-1}(x)),$$

and

$$\max(x,y) = d(\min(d(x),d(y))).$$

Hence $[\{sh\}] = P'_k$.

Thus we have the following completeness criterion: $M \subseteq P'_k$ is complete in P'_k if and only if $sh \in [M]$. This can be used to deduce the following theorem.

Theorem 3.2. The completeness of a finite subset of P'_k is decidable.

Proof. For $N \subseteq P'_k$, let

$$U(N) = \{f : f = \alpha(h \circ h') \in P'^2_k, \text{ where } \alpha \text{ is a composition of the operations } \zeta, \tau, \Delta, \nabla, \text{ and } h, h' \in N\}.$$

If N is finite, we can construct $U(N)$ effectively. Therefore the following diagram describes an algorithm to decide the completeness of a finite set $M \subseteq P'_k$.

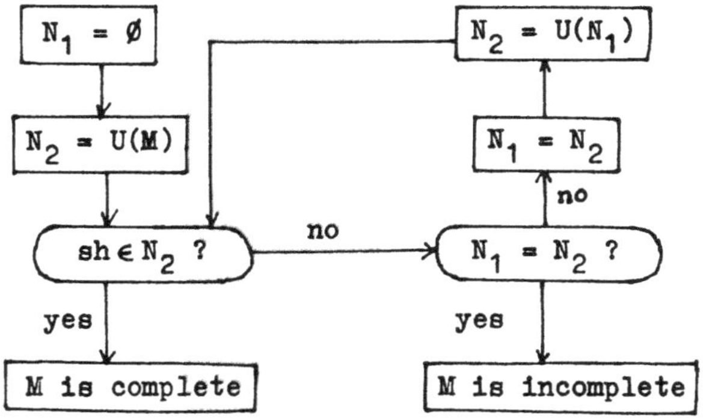

Figure 6

The algorithm stops after a finite number of steps since N_1 and N_2 contain only functions of P'^2_k and $|P'^2_k| = k^{k^2}$.

If we apply the above completeness criterion, we have to show that a fixed function (or a set of fixed functions) can be generated by M. Therefore we are interested in more general completeness criteria. We present two examples of the following type: M is complete if and only if it generates some (not fixed) functions with certain properties.

A function $f \in P_k'^n$ is called linear if it can be given in the form

$$f(x_1,x_2,\dots,x_n) = a_0 + a_1x_1 + a_2x_2 + \dots + a_nx_n \mod k$$

for some $a_0,a_1,\dots,a_n \in E_k$. L denotes the set of linear functions of P_2'.

We say that $f \in P_k'$ is semisimple if it essentially depends at most on one variable or if it is not surjective. S_k denotes the set of all semisimple functions of P_k'.

We put

$$N(k) = \begin{cases} L & \text{if } k = 2 \\ S_k & \text{if } k \geq 3 . \end{cases}$$

<u>Lemma 3.3.</u> i) If M contains all unary functions and a function $f \in N(k)$, then M is complete in $\underline{P_k'}$.

ii) If M contains a binary function f such that there is an $a \in E_k$ satisfying

a) $(E_k \setminus \{a\}, f)$ is a group,

b) $f(a,x) = f(x,a) = a$ for all $x \in E_k$,

and a unary function g such that

$$|\{g(0),\ g^2(0),\ \dots,\ g^k(0)\}| = k,$$

then M is complete.

The following theorem gives the most general completeness criterion.

<u>Theorem 3.4.</u> i) $M \subseteq P_k'$ is complete in $\underline{P_k'}$ if and only if it is not contained in any maximal subalgebra of $\underline{P_k'}$.

ii) $\underline{P_k'}$ has finitely many maximal subalgebras.

<u>Proof</u>. i) follows from Lemma 1.6..

ii) For a proper subset S of $P_k'^1$ we define

$$F(S) = \{f : f \in P_k',\ f(g_1(x),g_2(x),\dots,g_n(x)) \in S \text{ for all } g_i \in S\} .$$

It is easy to prove that $\underline{F(S)}$ is a proper subalgebra of $\underline{P_k'}$. Now let M be a proper subalgebra of P_k'. If $S = M \cap P_k'^1 \subsetneq P_k'^1$, then $M \subseteq F(S)$. Suppose that $M \cap P_k'^1 = P_k'^1$. Since M is not complete, we have $M \subseteq N(k)$ by Lemma 3.3.i). Hence the maximal subalgebras of $\underline{P_k'}$ can be represented in the form N(k) or F(S) for some proper subsets $S \subseteq P_k'^{1}$.

In order to get an applicable criterion we need an exact description of the maximal subalgebras.

Lemma 3.5. The maximal subalgebras of $\underline{P_2'}$ are given by the following carriers:

L,

$S = \{f : f(x_1,x_2,\dots,x_n) = \mathrm{cyc}(f(\mathrm{cyc}(x_1), \mathrm{cyc}(x_2),\dots,\mathrm{cyc}(x_n))\}$,

$\mathcal{M} = \{f : \text{if } a_i \le b_i \text{ for } 1 \le i \le n, \text{ then } f(a_1,a_2,\dots,a_n) \le f(b_1,b_2,\dots,b_n)\}$,

$T_0 = \{f : f(0,0,\dots,0) = 0\}$,

$T_1 = \{f : f(1,1,\dots,1) = 1\}$.

They are the sets of linear, selfdual, monotonous, 0-preserving, and 1-preserving functions, respectively. Note the following relations:

$$S = F(\{\mathrm{id}, \mathrm{cyc}\}),\ \mathcal{M} = F(\{\mathrm{id}, k_0, k_1\}),\ T_0 = F(\{k_0\}),\ T_1 = F(\{k_1\}),$$

where id denotes the function defined by $\mathrm{id}(x) = x$, $\mathrm{id} \in P_k'^{1}$. By Lemma 3.5. it is easy to characterize those functions that generate the algebra $\underline{P_2'}$.

Lemma 3.6. $\{f\}$ is complete in $\underline{P_2'}$ if and only if

$f(0,0,\dots,0) = 1$,

$f(1,1,\dots,1) = 0$, and

$f(a_1,a_2,\dots,a_n) = f(\mathrm{cyc}(a_1), \mathrm{cyc}(a_2), \dots, \mathrm{cyc}(a_n))$

for some $a_1,a_2,\dots,a_n \in E_2$.

For arbitrary $k \ge 2$, I. Rosenberg determined the maximal subalgebras of $\underline{P_k'}$. A result analogous to Lemma 3.6. was proved by V.B. Kudrjavcev and G. Rousseau for $k \ge 3$.
We now give statements which show differences between $\underline{P_2'}$ and $\underline{P_k'}$, $k \ge 3$.

Lemma 3.7. i) Let r_k denote the cardinality of the set of subalgebras of $\underline{P_k'}$. Then

$$r_k = \begin{cases} \aleph_0 & \text{if } k = 2 \\ \mathfrak{c} & \text{if } k \ge 3 \end{cases} \quad (\mathfrak{c} \text{ denotes the cardinality of } \mathbb{R}).$$

ii) Any subalgebra of $\underline{P_2'}$ is finitely generated.

iii) In P_k', $k \geq 3$, there are subalgebras M_1, M_2, and M_3 such that M_1 is finitely generated, M_2 has an infinite basis, M_3 has no basis.

In the following chapter we shall deal with the same problems in the algebra $\underline{P_k}$. It will become obvious that the algebraic and algorithmic structure of $\underline{P_k}$ is much more complicated than that of $\underline{P_k'}$.

Finally we note a property of functions of P_2'. Instead of max, min, and cyc we shall also use the notations vel, et, non. Then

$$et(x,y) = x \cdot y \mod 2.$$

Any function $f \in P_2'$ of arity n can be represented as a polynomial in at most n indeterminants, i.e.

$$f(x_1, x_2, \ldots, x_n) = U_1 + U_2 + \ldots + U_r + a \mod 2$$

for some $a \in E_2$, $U_i = x_{i_1} x_{i_2} \ldots x_{i_r} \mod 2$, $1 \leq i_j \leq n$, $1 \leq i \leq r$.

Exercises

1. Let aut denote the addition modulo 2. Prove the completeness of $\{et, aut, k_1\}$ in P_2'
   i) by generating vel and non,
   ii) by Theorem 3.5.,
   iii) by the algorithm of Theorem 3.2..
2. Prove Theorem 3.5. and Lemma 3.6.. (Hint: Discuss all possibilities for $F(S)$.)
3. $E \subseteq E_2{}^n$ is called 0-separating if and only if $E \subseteq E_2{}^{i-1} \times \{0\} \times E_2{}^{n-i}$ for some i. $f \in P_2'$ is called 0-separating of degree r iff each subset of $f^{-1}(\{0\})$ which consist of r elements is 0-separating. By $S(r)$ we denote the set of functions which are 0-separating of degree r. Prove the following statements:
   i) $\underline{S(r)}$ is a subalgebra of $\underline{P_2'}$.
   ii) $S(r) \supsetneqq S(r+1)$ for $r \geq 1$.
   Note that therefore $\underline{P_2'}$ contains an infinite chain of subalgebras (cf. /JGK/).
4. Prove: i) Any basis of $\underline{P_2}$ contains at most four functions.
   ii) For $1 \leq i \leq 4$ there is a basis for $\underline{P_2}$ consisting of i elements.

5. Let $0 \leq i \leq k-1$. Prove the maximality of the subalgebra $\underline{T_i}$ in $\underline{P'_k}$ where

$$T_i = \{f : f(i,i,i,\ldots,i) = i\}.$$

6. Show that $id \in M$ holds for any maximal subalgebra $\underline{M}$ of $\underline{P'_k}$.

7. Let $p \in P'^{3}_{k}$ be defined by

$$p(x,y,z) = \begin{cases} z & \text{if } y \neq z \\ x & \text{if } y = z. \end{cases}$$

Prove that $\{p, k_0, k_1, \ldots, k_{k-1}\}$ is complete in $\underline{P'_k}$ (cf. /We/ for the importance of p with respect to completeness in algebraic considerations).

8. Show that the maximal subalgebras of $\underline{T_0} \subseteq \underline{P'_2}$ are given by the carriers $T_0 \cap L$, $T_0 \cap S$, $T_0 \cap T_1$, and $S(2)$ (cf. /JGK/).

4. THE COMPLETENESS PROBLEM IN $\underline{P_k}$

4.1. Generation of $\underline{P_k}$ and its Subalgebras

By the definition of logical nets, Theorem 2.5., and the definition of the operations of our algebra we have that

$$\{F_{(\min)}, F_{(\max)}, F_{(cyc)}, F_{(id;1;0)}\}$$

is a system of generators for $\underline{P_k}$. This implies

Theorem 4.1. $\underline{P_k}$ is finitely generated.

The following statement gives an improved version of Lemma 1.2..

Theorem 4.2. For every natural number $n \geq 1$, there exists a basis for $\underline{P_k}$ which consists of exactly n functions.

Proof. i) $n = 1$, $k = 2$. We consider the function $F \in P_2{}^3$ defined by

$$\varphi^1_F(x_1(1),x_2(1),x_3(1)) = sh(x_1(1),x_2(1))$$

$$\varphi^t_F(x_1(1),x_2(1),x_3(1),\ldots,x_1(t),x_2(t),x_3(t)) = \min(sh(x_1(t),x_2(t)),x_3(t-1)) \quad \text{for} \quad t \geq 2,$$

and we define the sequential functions F_1, F_2, F_3, and F_4, by the Figures 7, 8, 9, 10, respectively. Then we obtain

$$F_1 = F_{(k_1)}, \quad F_2 = F_{(k_0)}, \quad F_3 = F_{(sh)}, \quad F_4 = F_{(id;1;0)}.$$

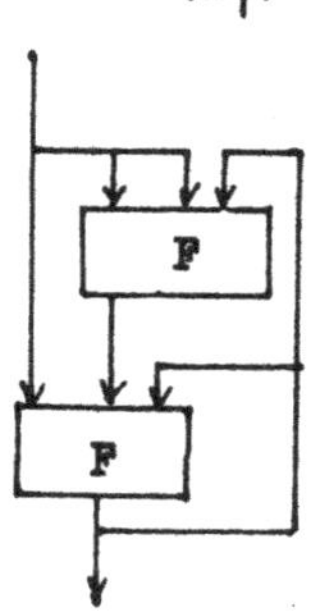

Figure 7

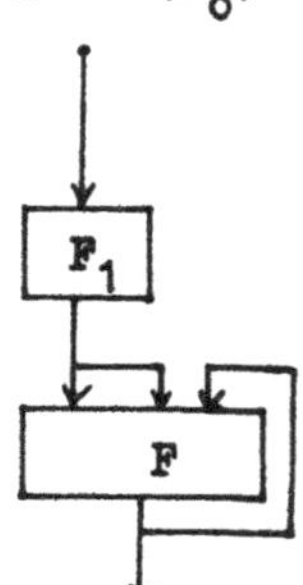

Figure 8

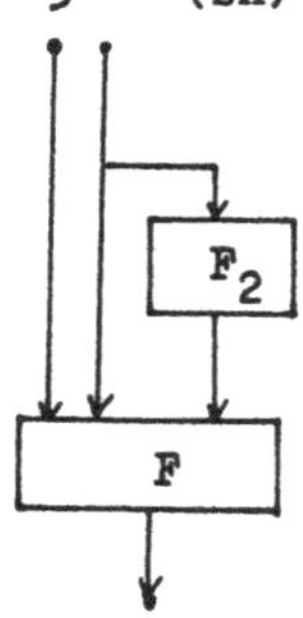

Figure 9

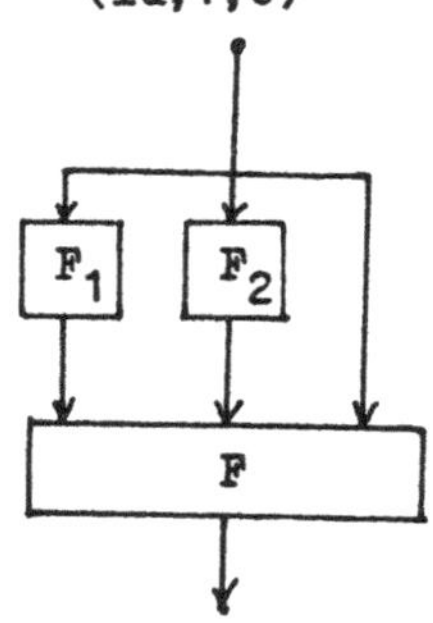

Figure 10

By the results of Chapter 3 we have

$$F_{(min)},\ F_{(max)},\ F_{(cyc)} \in [\{F_{(sh)}\}] \subseteq [\{F\}]$$

and as also

$$F_{(id;1;0)} \in [\{F\}],$$

the completeness of $\{F\}$ follows.

ii) $n = 1$, $k \geq 3$. Let F be the sequential function defined by

$$\varphi_F^t(x_1(1),\dots,x_5(1),\dots,x_1(t),\dots,x_5(t))$$

$$= \begin{cases} x_3(t) + 1 \mod k & \text{if } x_3(t) = x_4(t) \\ k-1 & \text{if } x_4(t) = x_3(t) + 1 \mod k \\ sh(x_1(t), x_2(t)) & \text{if } t = 1,\ x_3(t) \neq x_4(t) \neq x_3(t)+1 \\ \max(sh(x_1(t), x_2(t)), x_5(t-1)) & \text{otherwise.} \end{cases}$$

Then we generate the functions F_1, F_2, F_3, F_4 according to the Figures 11, 12, 13, 14, respectively. Then we have

$$F_1 = F_{(cyc)},\ F_2 = F_{(k_{k-1})},\ F_3 = F_{(sh)},\ F_4 = F_{(id;1;0)}.$$

Now the completeness follows as above.

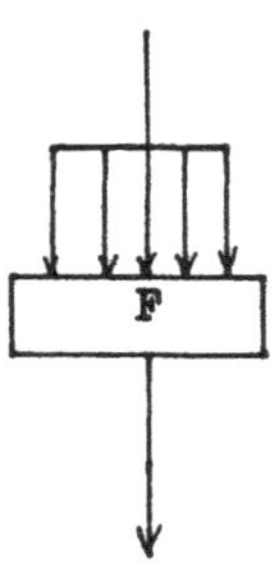

Figure 11

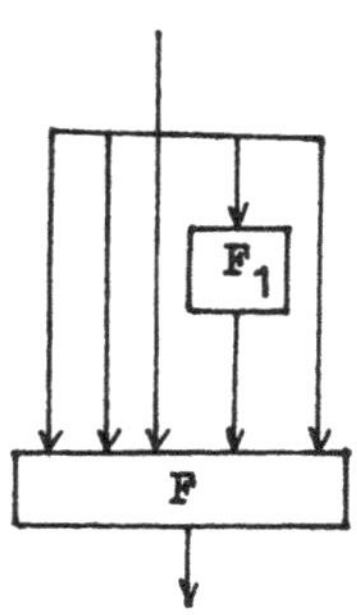

Figure 12

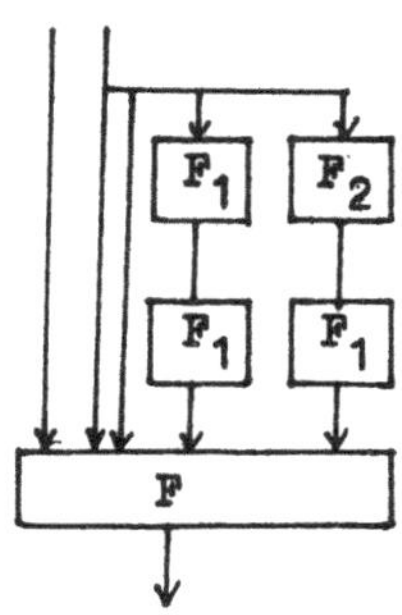

Figure 13

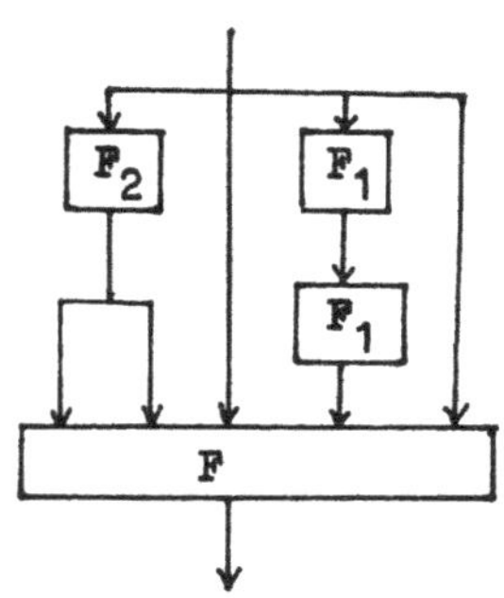

Figure 14

iii) $n = 2$, $k \geq 2$. $\{F_{(sh)}, F_{(id;1;0)}\}$ is complete. It is a basis since

$$F_{(sh)} \in M^2, \quad F_{(id;1;0)} \notin M^2,$$

$$F_{(sh)} \notin M_{T_0}, \quad F_{(id;1;0)} \in M_{T_0}.$$

iv) $n \geq 3$, $k \geq 2$. We consider the set $\{H_1, H_2, \ldots, H_n\}$ where

$$H_i \in P_k^{\,2} \quad \text{for} \quad 1 \leq i \leq n-1, \qquad H_n \in P_k^{\,1},$$

$$\varphi^t_{H_i}(x_1(1), x_2(1), \ldots, x_1(t), x_2(t)) = \begin{cases} x_1(t) & \text{for } i \neq t \\ sh(x_1(t), x_2(t)) & \text{for } i = t \end{cases}$$

for $1 \leq i \leq n-2$,

$$\varphi^t_{H_{n-1}}(x_1(1), x_2(1), \ldots, x_1(t), x_2(t)) = \begin{cases} x_1(t) & \text{for } t < i \\ sh(x_1(t), x_2(t)) & \text{for } t \geq i, \end{cases}$$

$$H_n = F_{(id;1;0)}.$$

This set is complete since $F_{(sh)} \in [\{H_1, H_2, \ldots, H_{n-1}\}]$ as shown in Figure 15. Further

$$\{H_1, H_2, \ldots, H_{n-1}\} \subseteq M^2, \qquad H_n \notin M^2,$$

$$\{H_1, H_2, \ldots, H_{i-1}, H_{i+1}, \ldots, H_n\} \subseteq N^i, \qquad H_i \notin N^i,$$

and this proves that $\{H_1, H_2, \ldots, H_n\}$ forms a basis.

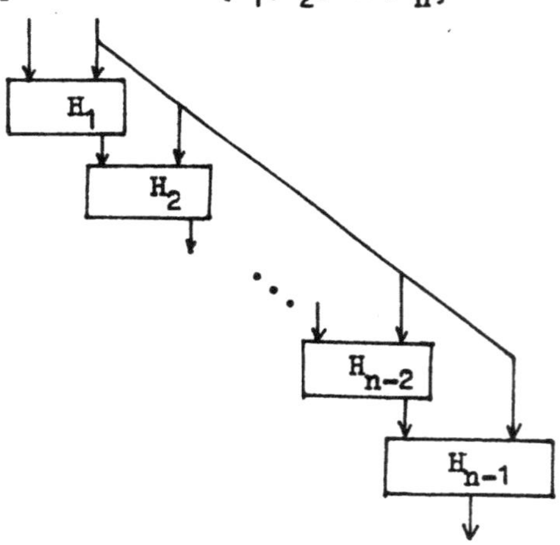

Figure 15

We have shown the existence of a sequential function F which generates $\underline{P_k}$. But the function used in the proof is complicated, for instance it has at least three input variables. Therefore we can ask whether or not there is a simpler function generating $\underline{P_k}$. Clearly, F has to have at least the weight 2 since a function F with weight 1 satisfies $F = F_{(f)}$ for some $f \in P_k'$. Further, F has to have at least two essential variables because the functions of $[\{F\}]$ have at most one essential variable in the opposite case. Therefore the simplest possible function F with $[\{F\}] = P_k$ has to have at least 2 input lines and weight 2. Without proof we give the result of Buevic that such a function exists.

Theorem 4.3. There exists a function $F \in P_k^2$ of weight 2 such that $[\{F\}] = P_k$.

In the proofs of Theorem 4.1. and Theorem 4.2. the feedback operation plays an important rule.(Note that we have also used it in the proof of Lemma 2.4..) In order to illustrate its importance we shall give some results on the algebra

$$\overline{\underline{P_k}} = (P_k; \zeta, \tau, \Delta, \circ, \nabla),$$

where feedback is not an operation. If we consider $\overline{\underline{P_k}}$, we shall use the following concepts and notations: s-subalgebra, s-complete, s-basis, $[M]_s$, etc.

Now we shall introduce some additional concepts, which will be needed later, too.

Z_k denotes the set of all periodic ω-words over E_k. In the sequel we use the following notation: If $\alpha \in Z_k$, then $\alpha = \alpha(1)\alpha(2)\ldots$ where $\alpha(1), \alpha(2), \ldots$ are the letters of α. For an ω-word α, we denote by $]\alpha[$ the set of all ω-words γ such that γ and α differ only in a finite number of letters, i.e. there is a number r such that $\gamma(s) = \alpha(s)$ for $r \leq s$. Note that $\alpha \in Z_k$ implies $\gamma \in Z_k$. For $Z' \subseteq Z_k$, we put

$$]Z'[\;=\; \bigcup_{\alpha \in Z'}]\alpha[\;.$$

Observe that the mapping $Z' \longrightarrow]Z'[$ is a closure operator. For $\alpha \in Z_k$, we define the constant sequential function C_α by

$$\varphi^t_{C_\alpha} = k_{\alpha(t)} \quad \text{for} \quad t \geq 1.$$

We say that the sequential function $F \in P_k^n$ preserves the set Z', $Z' \subseteq Z_k$, iff, for any ω-words $\alpha_1, \alpha_2, \ldots, \alpha_n \in Z'$, we have $F(\alpha_1, \alpha_2, \ldots, \alpha_n) \in Z'$. $M \subseteq P_k$ preserves Z' iff any function of M preserves Z'. Evidently, if a constant sequential mapping C_α preserves Z', then $\alpha \in Z'$, and conversely, if $\alpha \in Z'$, then C_α preserves Z'.

Lemma 4.4. The set of all sequential functions which preserves a subset of Z_k forms an s-subalgebra.

Proof. Let $F \in P_k^n$, $G \in P_k^m$ be functions preserving Z', $Z' \subseteq Z_k$. Let $\alpha_1, \alpha_2, \ldots, \alpha_{n+m-1} \in Z'$. Then

$$(\zeta F)(\alpha_1, \alpha_2, \ldots, \alpha_n) = F(\alpha_2, \alpha_3, \ldots, \alpha_n, \alpha_1) \in Z',$$

$$(\Delta F)(\alpha_1, \alpha_2, \ldots, \alpha_{n-1}) = F(\alpha_1, \alpha_1, \alpha_2, \alpha_3, \ldots, \alpha_{n-1}) \in Z',$$

and analogously for τ and ∇. Further $G(\alpha_1, \alpha_2, \ldots, \alpha_m) = \beta \in Z'$ and

$$(F \circ G)(\alpha_1, \alpha_2, \ldots, \alpha_{n+m-1}) = F(G(\alpha_1, \ldots, \alpha_m), \alpha_{m+1}, \ldots, \alpha_{m+n-1}))$$
$$= F(\beta, \alpha_{m+1}, \alpha_{m+2}, \ldots, \alpha_{m+n-1})) \in Z'.$$

We notice that the following statement does not hold in general: If F preserves Z', then $\times F$ preserves Z'. We consider the following example. Let $F \in P_k^2$ be defined by

$$\varphi_F^1 = k_0, \quad \varphi_F^t(x_1(1), x_2(1), \ldots, x_1(t), x_2(t)) = x_1(t-1) \quad \text{for} \quad t \geq 2.$$

Then $\times F = C_\alpha$ with $\alpha = 00\ldots$. Clearly, F preserves the set

$$Z' = \{ \beta : \beta(1) = \beta(2) = \ldots = \beta(r) = 0,$$
$$1 = \beta(r+1) = \beta(r+2) = \ldots \quad \text{for some} \quad r \geq 1 \},$$

but Z' is not preserved by $\times F$.

Theorem 4.5. Any s-complete set is infinite.

Proof. Suppose there is a finite s-complete set M. Then there is a number n such that the weight of each element of M is smaller than n. Let $p_1, p_2, \ldots, p_k$ be the prime numbers smaller than n, and let H_n be the set of all periodic ω-words with a period m such that

$$m = p_1^{s_1} p_2^{s_2} \ldots p_k^{s_k}$$

for some $s_1, s_2, \ldots, s_k \in \mathbb{N}$. We prove that any function of $[M]_s$ preserves H_n. By Lemma 4.4., we only have to prove that any sequential function of M preserves H_n. Let $F \in M$, $F \in P_k^r$, and $\alpha_1, \alpha_2, \ldots, \alpha_r$ be ω-words of H_n. Let $q_1, q_2, \ldots, q_r$ be the periods of $\alpha_1, \alpha_2, \ldots, \alpha_r$, respectively. Then the ω-word

$$\alpha = (\alpha_1(1), \alpha_2(1), \ldots, \alpha_r(1))(\alpha_1(2), \alpha_2(2), \ldots, \alpha_r(2)) \ldots$$

over E_k^n is periodic with the period $q = q_1 q_2 \ldots q_r$. By Lemma 2.7., we obtain that $F(\alpha)$ is also periodic and its period is uq, where u is smaller than the weight of F. Therefore $u \leq n$ and u has a representation

$$u = p_1^{u_1} p_2^{u_2} \ldots p_k^{u_k}$$

for some $u_1, u_2, \ldots, u_k \in \mathbb{N}$. Since each q_i, $1 \leq i \leq r$, has this form, too, we have $F(\alpha) \in H_n$.
Now, let p_{k+1} be the next prime number and γ the ω-word

$$\gamma = \underbrace{000\ldots001}_{\substack{p_{k+1}\\ \text{letters}}}\underbrace{000\ldots001}_{\substack{p_{k+1}\\ \text{letters}}}\underbrace{000\ldots001}_{\substack{p_{k+1}\\ \text{letters}}}\ldots$$

Then C_γ does not preserve H_n and thus $C_\gamma \in [M]_s$. This proves the incompleteness of M.

Let $F \in P_k^n$ and $\alpha \in Z_k$. We say that the i-th variable of F has the $\mathcal{F}$-property with respect to α iff there are natural numbers t_1, t_2 (which depend only on F and α) such that, for all $\alpha_1, \alpha_2, \ldots, \alpha_n$ with $\alpha_i(s) = \alpha(s)$ for $s > t_1$, we have

$$F(\alpha_1, \alpha_2, \ldots, \alpha_n)(r) = \alpha(r) \quad \text{for} \quad r > t_2.$$

The i-th variable of F has the $\mathcal{F}$-property with respect to $Z' \subseteq Z_k$ if this variable has the $\mathcal{F}$-property with respect to each $\alpha \in Z'$.
If a variable of C_α has the $\mathcal{F}$-property on Z', then

$$C_\alpha(\alpha_1, \alpha_2, \ldots, \alpha_n) = \alpha \in \,]Z'[\,.$$

<u>Lemma 4.6.</u> Let Z' be a subset of Z_k such that $Z' = \,]Z'[\,$. If a variable of F has the $\mathcal{F}$-property with respect to Z', then F preserves Z'.

<u>Proof</u>. Without loss of generality let the first variable have the $\mathcal{F}$-property on Z'. Let $\alpha_1, \alpha_2, \ldots, \alpha_n \in Z'$, where n is the arity of F. Then $F(\alpha_1, \alpha_2, \ldots, \alpha_n) \in \,]\alpha_1[\,$ by the definition of the $\mathcal{F}$-property, and hence $F(\alpha_1, \alpha_2, \ldots, \alpha_n) \in Z'$.

<u>Lemma 4.7.</u> For any sequential function $F \in P_2^n$ and any periodic ω-word β there is a sequential function $T_{\beta,F} \in P_2^{n+1}$ such that

i) $T_{\beta,F}(\beta, \alpha_1, \alpha_2, \ldots, \alpha_n) = F(\alpha_1, \alpha_2, \ldots, \alpha_n)$,

ii) the first variable of $T_{\beta,F}$ has the $\mathcal{F}$-property on each ω-word different from β.

Proof. We consider the net of Figure 16 where

$$f(x_1,x_2,x_3) = \mathrm{vel}(\mathrm{et}(\mathrm{non}(x_1),x_2),\mathrm{et}(x_1,x_3)).$$

If the input on the first line is β, then the output of $F_{(eq)}$ [1] is identically 1, and thus the input of $F_{(f)}$ on its first line is also 1 at every time moment. Therefore $F_{(f)}$ emits the input of its third input line, i.e.

$$T_{\beta,F}(\beta,\alpha_1,\alpha_2,\ldots,\alpha_n) = F(\alpha_1,\alpha_2,\ldots,\alpha_n).$$

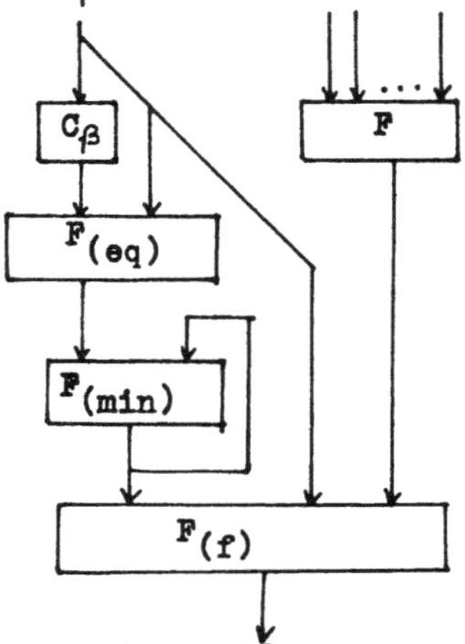

Figure 16

Let $\alpha \neq \beta$. Then there is a number t such that

$$\alpha(i) = \beta(i) \quad \text{for} \quad i < t,$$
$$\alpha(t) \neq \beta(t).$$

If the first source emits the ω-word α, then the output of $F_{(\mathrm{non} \circ \mathrm{aut})}$ at the t-th moment is 0. Therefore the input of $F_{(f)}$ on its first input line is the ω-word

$$\underbrace{11\ldots11}_{\substack{t-1\\ \text{times}}}000\ldots \quad .$$

Hence

$$T_{\beta,F}(\alpha,\alpha_1,\alpha_2,\ldots,\alpha_n)(r) = \alpha(r) \quad \text{for} \quad r > t.$$

We choose $t_1(\alpha,T_{\beta,F}) = t_2(\alpha,T_{\beta,F}) = t$ and have proved that the first variable of $T_{\beta,F}$ has $\mathcal{F}$-property on α.

Lemma 4.8. There is an s-complete set M such that any subset M' of M with $[M']_s = P_k$ is reducible.

Proof. With an integer s, $1 \leq s \leq k^i$, we associate the i-tuple $(\delta_1^s, \delta_2^s, \ldots, \delta_i^s)$ such that

$$s - 1 = \sum_{j=1}^{i} \delta_{i-j+1}^{s} \cdot k^{j-1}.$$

We consider the logical nets with $k^i + ik^i$ input lines corresponding

---

[1] $\mathrm{eq}(x,y) = \mathrm{non}(x + y \mod 2)$

to the variables

$$u_1, u_2, \ldots, u_{k^i}, \; x_1, x_2, \ldots, x_{k^i}, x_{k^i+1}, \ldots, x_{ik^i}$$

and the following canonical system of equations: For $r = 1,2,\ldots,i$, $t \geq 1$,

$$q_r(0) = 0$$

$$q_r(t) = \max_{1 \leq s \leq k^i} \min(u_{\delta_1^s}(q_1(t-1)), \ldots, u_{\delta_i^s}(q_i(t-1)), \; x_{r+(s-1)i}(t))$$

$$y(t) = \max_{1 \leq s \leq k^i} \min(u_{\delta_1^s}(q_1(t-1)), \ldots, u_{\delta_i^s}(q_i(t-1)), \; u_s(t))$$

(for the definition of $u_i(x)$ we refer to the proof of Theorem 3.1.). Let F_i be the sequential function which is induced by this net. We choose

$$M = \{ F_{(sh)}, F_1, F_2, \ldots, F_i, \ldots \}.$$

First we prove the s-completeness of M. Let F be an arbitrary sequential function of weight n with m variables. Let $k^{i-1} < n \leq k^i$. Then the logical net corresponding to F can be described by the following canonical system of equations: For $r = 1,2,\ldots,i$, $t \geq 1$,

$$q_r(0) = 0,$$

$$q_r(t) = \varphi_r(q_1(t-1), q_2(t-1), \ldots, q_i(t-1), x_1(t), x_2(t), \ldots, x_m(t)),$$

$$y(t) = \psi(q_1(t-1), q_2(t-1), \ldots, q_i(t-1), x_1(t), x_2(t), \ldots, x_m(t)).$$

The functions φ_r, $r = 1,2,\ldots,i$, and ψ can be represented in the form (this representation is analogous to the representation in the proof of Lemma 2.4.)

$$\varphi_r(q_1, q_2, \ldots, q_i, x_1, x_2, \ldots, x_m) = \max_{1 \leq s \leq k^i} \min(u_{\delta_1^s}(q_1), \ldots, u_{\delta_i^s}(q_i), \; \varphi_r^{(s)}(x_1, x_2, \ldots, x_m)),,$$

$$\psi(q_1, q_2, \ldots, q_i, x_1, x_2, \ldots, x_m) = \max_{1 \leq s \leq k^i} \min(u_{\delta_1^s}(q_1), \ldots, u_{\delta_i^s}(q_i), \; \psi^{(s)}(x_1, x_2, \ldots, x_m)).$$

The functions $F_{(\varphi_r^{(s)})}$ and $F_{(\psi^{(s)})}$, $r = 1,2,\ldots,i$, $s = 1,2,\ldots,k^i$,

can be generated by $F_{(sh)}$. If we substitute this functions for the variables $x_{r+(s-1)i}$ and u_s of F_i, we obtain F, and thus M is s-complete.
We now prove that any system M' of generators of P_k contained in M is reducible. Obviously, $F_{(sh)}$ has to be in M since φ_F^1 depends essentially on at most one variable for $F \in M'$, $F \neq F_{(sh)}$. Since M' is infinite by Theorem 4.5., we have $F_i, F_j \in M'$ with $i < j$. Now our above proof shows that $F_i \in [\{F_{(sh)}, F_j\}]_s$ and therefore M' is reducible.

<u>Lemma 4.9.</u> P_2 has an s-basis.

Proof. We inductively construct a basis $\{F_0', F_1', \ldots\}$ starting with the set $\{F_{(sh)}, F_1, F_2, \ldots\}$ of the proof of Lemma 4.8.. We define $F_0' = F_{(sh)}$. Let $\beta_1 = 00\ldots$ be an ω-word. We define $F_1' = T_{\beta_1, F_1}$. Let C_0 be the set of all ω-words with period 1. The set $[\{F_0', F_1'\}]_s$ has the following properties:

i) $[\{F_{(sh)}, F_1\}]_s \subseteq [\{F_0', F_1'\}]_s$

since $F_0' = F_{(sh)}$, $C_{\beta_1} \in [\{F_{(sh)}\}]_s$, and $F_1 = F_1' \circ C_{\beta_1}$,

ii) there is a constant sequential function $C_{\beta_2} \in [\{F_0', F_1'\}]_s$ such that $C_{\beta_2} \notin [\{F_0'\} \cup C_0]_s$.

The latter fact follows since F_1 has weight 2, and therefore we can generate any function with weight ≤ 2, especially the constant C_{β_2} with $\beta_2 = 1010\ldots$ (see the proof of Lemma 4.8.), which is not in $[\{F_0'\} \cup C_0]_s$ because all constants of this set are already in C_0. Suppose that we have already constructed $F_0', F_1', \ldots, F_n'$ such that

i) $[\{F_{(sh)}, F_1, F_2, \ldots, F_n\}]_s \subseteq [\{F_0', F_1', \ldots, F_n'\}]_s$

and

ii) there is a constant $C_{\beta_{n+1}}$ such that

$$C_{\beta_{n+1}} \in [\{F_0', F_1', \ldots, F_n'\}]_s, \quad C_{\beta_{n+1}} \notin [\{F_0', F_1', \ldots, F_{n-1}'\} \cup C_0]_s .$$

We consider $G_{n+1} = T_{\beta_{n+1}, F_{n+1}}$. If any constant of $[\{F_0', F_1', \ldots, F_n', G_{n+1}\}]_s$ is already in $[\{F_0', F_1', \ldots, F_n'\} \cup C_0]_s$, we put $G_{n+2} = T_{\beta_{n+1}, F_{n+2}}$. We continue this process until we find a number t

such that there is a function $C_{\beta_{n+2}}$ with

$$C_{\beta_{n+2}} \in [\{F'_0, F'_1, \dots, F'_n, G_{n+1}, G_{n+2}, \dots, G_{n+t}\}]_s$$

$$C_{\beta_{n+2}} \notin [\{F'_0, F'_1, \dots, F'_n, G_{n+1}, G_{n+2}, \dots, G_{n+t-1}\} \cup C_o]_s .$$

Such a number t has to exist since any set

$$[\{F'_0, F'_1, \dots, F'_n, G_{n+1}, G_{n+2}, \dots, G_{n+i}\}]_s$$

preserves a set H_r for some r (for H_r we refer to the proof of Theorem 4.5.), and we can construct C_γ such that the period of γ is sufficiently large using $F_{n+j} = G_{n+j} \circ C_{\beta_{n+1}}$ with sufficiently large j. We put

$$F'_{n+1} = G_{n+t} = T_{\beta_{n+1}, F_{n+t}} .$$

Then

i) $[\{F_{(sh)}, F_1, F_2, \dots, F_{n+1}\}]_s \subseteq [\{F'_0, F'_1, \dots, F'_{n+1}\}]_s$

by $F_{n+t} = F'_{n+1} \circ C_{\beta_{n+1}}$, $F'_0 = F_{(sh)}$, and the proof of Lemma 4.8., and

ii) there exists a constant $C_{\beta_{n+2}}$ such that

$$C_{\beta_{n+2}} \in [\{F'_0, F'_1, \dots, F'_{n+1}\}]_s, \quad C_{\beta_{n+2}} \notin [\{F'_0, F'_1, \dots, F'_n\} \cup C_o]_s .$$

By the construction, we have

$$P_2 = [\{F_{(sh)}, F_1, F_2, \dots\}]_s \subseteq [\{F'_0, F'_1, \dots\}]_s ,$$

i.e. the completeness is proved.
We prove the incompleteness of $\{F'_0, F'_1, \dots, F'_{i-1}, F'_{i+1}, F'_{i+2}, \dots\}$ for $i \geq 1$. Let C_j be the set of all constant sequential functions in $[\{F'_0, F'_1, \dots, F'_j\}]_s$ and put

$$Z'_j = \{\alpha : C_\alpha \in C_j\} .$$

We remark $Z'_j = \,]Z'_j[$. This can be proved as follows. Let $\alpha \in \,]Z'_j[$ and $\alpha' \in Z'_j$ such that $\alpha(s) = \alpha'(s)$ for $s \geq r$. We define the ω-word α'' by

$$\alpha''(i) = 0 \text{ if and only if } \alpha(i) = \alpha'(i).$$

Then $C_{\alpha''} \in C_o \subseteq C_j$, and since $C_\alpha \in C_j$, and the function F with

$$F(p) = F_{(f)}(C_\alpha(p), C_{\alpha''}(p)) ,$$

where

$$f(x,y) = \begin{cases} x & \text{if } y = 0 \\ cyc(x) & \text{if } y = 1 \end{cases}$$

coincides with $C_{\alpha'}$, we obtain $C_{\alpha'} \in C_j$, i.e. $\alpha' \in Z_j'$.
Now it is obvious that F_0', $F_1', \dots, F_j'$ preserve the set Z_j'. Further, $\beta_i \notin Z_j'$ for $i \geq j+1$ by construction. Therefore the first variable of F_i', $i \geq j+1$, has the $\mathcal{F}$-property on Z_j'. Thus F_i', $i \geq j+1$, preserves Z_j' by Lemma 4.6.. Therefore

$$[\{F_0', F_1', \dots, F_{i-1}', F_{i+1}', F_{i+2}', \dots\}]_s$$

preserves Z_{i-1}'. This proves the incompleteness.
Now, if $F_0' \notin [\{F_1', F_2', \dots\}]_s$, then $\{F_0', F_1', F_2', \dots\}$ forms an s-basis.
If $F_0' \in [\{F_1', F_2', \dots\}]_s$, then $\{F_1', F_2', \dots\}$ forms an s-basis.

Combining Lemma 4.8. and Lemma 4.9. we have

Theorem 4.10. $\underline{\overline{P_2}}$ is of type 4.

Concluding this paragraph we show that subalgebras of $\underline{P_k}$ can have a more complicated structure than $\underline{P_k}$ with respect to its generation by subsets (compare with Lemma 3.7.,too).

Theorem 4.11. Let $i \in \{1,2,3,4\}$. Then there exists a subalgebra $\underline{M_i}$ of $\underline{P_k}$ such that $\underline{M_i}$ is of type i.

Proof. We prove the theorem for $k = 2$ only (for $k \geq 3$ we have to use slight modifications).
i = 1. We take $\underline{M_1} = \underline{P_2}$.
i = 3. Let $C \subseteq P_k^{\,0}$ be an infinite set. We consider $M_2 = [C]$ (see example 2.11.). Let M be a system of generators for $\underline{M_2}$. Evidently, for every $G \in C$, M contains a function F such that $F = \nabla^n G$ for some n. We put

$$n(G) = \min\{n : \nabla^n G \in M\}.$$

Then

$$M' = \{\nabla^{n(G)}(G) : G \in C\}$$

is a subset of M and M' is a basis for M_2 as can be seen easily.

i = 2. We consider the set M_3 which consists of the constants $F_{(k_o)}$ of the arities 0,1,2,... and all functions $F \in P_k$ which can be given by

$$k_o = \varphi_F^1 = \varphi_F^3 = \varphi_F^4 = \dots ,$$

$$\varphi_F^2(x_1(1),x_2(1),\dots,x_n(1),x_1(2),x_2(2),\dots,x_n(2)) = \\ = \min(x_{i_1}(1),x_{i_2}(1),\dots,x_{i_r}(1))$$

where $\{i_1,i_2,\dots,i_r\} \subseteq \{1,2,\dots,n\}$ and n denotes the arity of F. It is easy to prove that $[M_3] = M_3$.
It is obvious that all operations do not increase the number of essential variables. Thus any system M of generators of M_3 has to contain a function F with $r_n > n$ variables for any $n \geq 1$. Therefore M contains at least two functions F_1, F_2 with different numbers n_1 and n_2 of essential variables. Let $n_1 > n_2$. Then F_1 generates F_2 using $n_1 - n_2$ times the operation Δ, appropriate permutations of variables and adding of dummy variables in order to get the correct number and correct order of the variables. Thus $M \setminus \{F_2\}$ is also complete. Hence any system of generators for M_3 is reducible.
i = 4. With $F \in P_2{}^n$ we associate the function $F' \in P_2{}^n$ defined by

$$\varphi_{F'}^1(x_1(1),x_2(1),\dots,x_n(1)) = et(x_1(1),x_2(1),\dots,x_n(1)),$$

$$\varphi_{F'}^t(x_1(1),x_2(1),\dots,x_n(1),\dots,x_1(t),x_2(t),\dots,x_n(t)) \\ = \varphi_F^{t-1}(x_1(2),\dots,x_n(2),\dots, x_1(t),\dots,x_n(t)), \ t \geq 2,$$

and we consider the set

$$M_4 = \{F' : F \in P_k\}.$$

M_4 is a subalgebra since $\alpha F' = (\alpha F)'$ for $\alpha \in \{\zeta, \tau, \Delta, \nabla\}$, $(F \circ G)' = F' \circ G'$, and the feedback is not applicable. Moreover, if $M \subseteq P_2$ is a system of generators of P_2 with respect to the operations $\zeta, \tau, \Delta, \nabla, \circ$, then $M' = \{F' : F \in M\}$ is a system of generators for $\underline{M_4}$, and M is reducible if and only if M' is reducible.
By Theorem 4.10., $\underline{M_4}$ is of type 4.

4.2. Maximal Subalgebras

By Theorem 4.1. and Lemma 1.6., we have the algebraic criterion for completeness.

Theorem 4.12. A set $M \subseteq P_k$ is complete in $\underline{P_k}$ if and only if it is not contained in any maximal subalgebra of $\underline{P_k}$.

Therefore it is of interest to have some knowledge of maximal subalgebras of $\underline{P_k}$. We give two examples.

Example 4.1. If $\underline{R}$ is a maximal subalgebra of $\underline{P_k'}$, then $\underline{M_R}$ is a maximal subalgebra of $\underline{P_k}$.

Proof. If $F \in M_R$, then $\varphi_F^1 \in R$. Since $\underline{R}$ is maximal in $\underline{P_k'}$, we have

$$[R \cup \{\varphi_F^1\}] = P_k' .$$

Because

$$\varphi_{\alpha F}^1 = \alpha \varphi_F^1 \quad \text{for} \quad \alpha \in \{\zeta, \tau, \Delta, \nabla\} \quad \text{and} \quad \varphi_{F \circ G}^1 = \varphi_F^1 \circ \varphi_G^1 ,$$

for any $f \in P_k'$, we have a sequential function $G(f)$ in $[M_R \cup \{F\}]$ such that $\varphi_{G(f)}^1 = f$.

Now let $H \in P_k$. Since $id \in R$, we have $H_1 \in M_R$ where

$$\varphi_{H_1}^1 = id \quad \text{and} \quad \varphi_{H_1}^t = \varphi_H^t \quad \text{for} \quad t \geq 2.$$

Thus $H_1 \in [M_R \cup \{F\}]$. Further, let F_1 be the sequential function defined by

$$\varphi_{F_1}^1(x_1(1), x_2(1)) = x_1(1),$$

$$\varphi_{F_1}^t(x_1(1), x_2(1), \ldots, x_1(t), x_2(t)) = x_2(t) \quad \text{for} \quad t \geq 2.$$

Obviously, $F_1 \in M_R \subseteq [M_R \cup \{F\}]$. Then the function H' with

$$H'(p_1, p_2, \ldots, p_n) = F_1(G(\varphi_H^1)(p_1, p_2, \ldots, p_n), H_1(p_1, p_2, \ldots, p_n))$$

is an element of $[M_R \cup \{F\}]$ and satisfies $H' = H$. Thus the completeness of $M_R \cup \{F\}$ is shown.

Example 4.2. M^2 is a maximal subalgebra of $\underline{P_2}$.

Proof. Assume $F \in M^2$. Then φ_F^2 depends essentially on $x_i(1)$ for some i, $1 \leq i \leq n$. Hence there are values a_{1j}, a_{2j} for $1 \leq j \leq n$, $j \neq i$, and a_{2i} such that

$$\varphi^2_F(a_{11},a_{12},\dots a_{1,i-1},x_i(1),a_{1,i+1},\dots,a_{1n},a_{21},a_{22},\dots,a_{2n})$$
$$= f(x_i(1)),$$

and f depends essentially on $x_i(1)$. Therefore $f\in\{\text{id}, \text{non}\}$.
For $1\le j\le n$, $j\ne i$, by G_j we denote a (fixed) function of P_k^1 which satisfies

$$\varphi^1_{G_j} = k_{a_{1j}}, \quad \varphi^2_{G_j} = k_{a_{2j}},$$

and let G_i be a function with

$$\varphi^1_{G_i} = f^{-1}, \quad \varphi^2_{G_i} = k_{a_{2i}}.$$

Then $G_l\in M^2$ for $1\le l\le n$, and the function F' given by

$$F(G_1(p),G_2(p),\dots,G_n(p)) = F'(p)$$

satisfies

$$F'\in[M^2\cup\{F\}] \quad \text{and} \quad \varphi^2_{F'}(x(1),x(2)) = x(1).$$

We define the sequential functions $F_2\in P_k{}^2$, $F_3\in P_k{}^1$ by

$$\varphi^1_{F_2}(x_1(1),x_2(1)) = x_1(1),$$

$$\varphi^2_{F_2}(x_1(1),x_2(1),x_1(2),x_2(2)) = x_2(2),$$

$$\varphi^t_{F_2}(x_1(1),x_2(1),\dots,x_1(t),x_2(t)) = x_1(t) \quad \text{for} \quad t\ge 3,$$

$$\varphi^1_{F_3} = \varphi^2_{F_3} = k_0,$$

$$\varphi^t_{F_3}(x(1),x(2),\dots,x(t)) = x(t-1) \quad \text{for} \quad t\ge 3.$$

Then F_2, $F_3\in M^2$. Further we have $H\in[M^2\cup\{F\}]$ where

$$H(p) = F_2(F_3(p),F'(p)).$$

$H = F_{(\text{id};1;0)}$ holds, too. Because $F_{(\text{sh})}\in M^2$ we obtain $[M^2\cup\{F\}] = P_k$. This proves the maximality of $\underline{M^2}$ in $\underline{P_k}$.

<u>Lemma 4.13.</u> Any maximal subalgebra of $\underline{P_k}$ contains all projections.

<u>Proof</u>. Assume $E\not\subseteq M$ for some maximal subalgebra $\underline{M}$. Then $F\notin M$ for some projection F, $F(p_1,p_2,\dots,p_n) = p_i$. If M contains a $G\in E$,

then $F \in [G] \subseteq M$ (see example 2.13.). Hence $E \cap M = \emptyset$. By the maximality of $\underline{M}$ and Lemma 2.9., $P_k = M \cup E$. Therefore $M = P_k \setminus E$. Thus $F_{(et)} \in M$ and $\Delta F_{(et)} = F_{(id)} \in M$. We now have a contradiction.

Unfortunately, the completeness criterion of Theorem 4.12. is not effective since the number of maximal subalgebras is infinite by Lemma 1.8. and Theorem 4.2.. More precisely, we have

Theorem 4.14. The cardinality of the set of all maximal subalgebras of $\underline{P_k}$ is $\mathfrak{c}$.

Proof. For the sake of simplicity we prove this theorem for $k = 2$.

Claim 1. Let $Z' \subseteq Z_2$. The set of all sequential functions which have a variable with $\mathcal{F}$-property on $]Z'[$ forms a subalgebra of $\underline{P_2}$.

Proof of claim 1. i) Let the i-th variable of $F \in P_2{}^n$ have the $\mathcal{F}$-property on $]Z'[$, $\alpha \in]Z'[$, and let $t_1 = t_1(F, \alpha)$ and $t_2 = t_2(F, \alpha)$ be the numbers of the definition of the $\mathcal{F}$-property with respect to α. Let α_i be an ω-word such that $\alpha_i(s) = \alpha(s)$ for $s \geq t_1$. Then

$$F(\alpha_1, \alpha_2, \ldots, \alpha_i, \ldots, \alpha_n)(r) = \alpha_i(r) \quad \text{for} \quad r > t_2.$$

Therefore

$$(\zeta F)(\alpha_1, \alpha_2, \ldots, \alpha_n)(r) = F(\alpha_2, \alpha_1, \alpha_3, \ldots, \alpha_n)(r) = \alpha_j(r)$$

for $r \geq t_2$ where

$$j = \begin{cases} i & \text{for} \quad i \geq 3 \\ 2 & \text{for} \quad i = 1 \\ 1 & \text{for} \quad i = 2. \end{cases}$$

Hence the j-th variable of ζF has the $\mathcal{F}$-property on α.
ii) An analogous proof can be given for τ, Δ, and ∇.
iii) Let $H = F \circ G$ where the i-th and j-th variable of F and G, respectively, have the $\mathcal{F}$-property on $]Z'[$. Obviously, if $i \geq 2$, then the $(m+i-1)$-th variable of $F \circ G$ has the $\mathcal{F}$-property on $]Z'[$. If $i = 1$, we prove that the j-th variable of $F \circ G$ has the $\mathcal{F}$-property on $]Z'[$. Let $\alpha \in]Z'[$, $t_1 = t_1(G, \alpha)$, and $t_2 = t_2(G, \alpha)$. Without loss of generality we can suppose that $t_1 < t_2$. Then

$$G(\alpha_1, \alpha_2, \ldots, \alpha_m)(r) = \alpha(r) \quad \text{for} \quad r > t_2$$

if $\alpha_j(s) = \alpha(s)$ for $s > t_1$. Let Z'' be the set of all words which differ from α at most in the first t_2 letters. By Lemma 4.6.,

$Z'' \subseteq]Z'[$. Let $t' = \max \{t_2(F, \beta) : \beta \in Z''\}$. Then, for arbitrary $\alpha_1, \alpha_2, \ldots, \alpha_m, \alpha_{m+1}, \ldots, \alpha_{m+n-1}$ such that $\alpha_j(s) = \alpha(s)$ for $s > t_1$,

$$(F \circ G)(\alpha_1, \alpha_2, \ldots, \alpha_{n+m-1})(r)$$
$$= F(G(\alpha_1, \alpha_2, \ldots, \alpha_m), \alpha_{m+1}, \alpha_{m+2}, \ldots, \alpha_{m+n-1})(r)$$
$$= \alpha(r) \quad \text{for} \quad r > t',$$

i.e. the j-th variable of $F \circ G$ has the $\mathcal{F}$-property on $]Z'[$.
iv) If F depends delayed on its first variable, the first variable cannot have the $\mathcal{F}$-property on $]Z'[$. If the i-th variable of F, $i \geq 2$, has the $\mathcal{F}$-property on $]Z'[$, then the (i-1)-th variable of $\times F$ has the $\mathcal{F}$-property on $]Z'[$.

The sequential function $F \in P_2^n$ is called almost constant iff there is a number t, which depends only on F, such that, for all ω-words $\alpha_1, \alpha_2, \ldots, \alpha_n, \gamma_1, \gamma_2, \ldots, \gamma_n$, we have

$$F(\alpha_1, \alpha_2, \ldots, \alpha_n)(s) = F(\gamma_1, \gamma_2, \ldots, \gamma_n)(s) \quad \text{for} \quad s \geq t.$$

Claim 2. The set of all almost constant functions of P_2 forms a subalgebra of $\underline{P_2}$.

The proof is left to the reader as an exercise.

Let $Z' \subseteq Z_2$, $Z' \neq \emptyset$. $U(Z')$ denotes the set of all functions $F \in P_2$ such that

i) F is almost constant and preserves $]Z'[$

or

ii) there is a variable of F which has the $\mathcal{F}$-property with respect to $]Z'[$.

Claim 3. i) $U(Z')$ preserves $]Z'[$.

ii) $U(Z') \cap \{C_\alpha : \alpha \in Z\} = \{C_\alpha : \alpha \in]Z'[\}$.

Proof of claim 3. i) follows from Lemma 4.6..
ii) Let C_α be a constant in $U(Z')$. If C_α preserves $]Z'[$, then $\alpha \in]Z'[$. If a variable of C_α has the $\mathcal{F}$-property on $]Z'[$, then $\alpha \in]]Z'[[=]Z'[$.
Conversely, any constant C_α with $\alpha \in]Z'[$ preserves $]Z'[$ and is almost constant.

Claim 4. If $Z' \subseteq Z_2$, then $U(Z')$ forms a subalgebra of $\underline{P_2}$.

Proof of claim 4. By Claim 1, Claim 2, and Lemma 4.4., we have to consider the following cases: $F \circ G$ and $G \circ F$ where the i-th variable of $F \in P_2^n$ has the $\mathcal{F}$-property with respect to $]Z'[$ and

$G \in P_2^m$ is almost constant and preserves $]Z'[$, and $\times G$ where G satisfies the same assumptions.

If $i \geq 2$, then the $(m+i-1)$-th variable of $F \circ G$ has the $\mathcal{F}$-property on $]Z'[$. Let $i = 1$. If $\alpha_1 \in]Z'[$, then there is an integer t and an ω-word $\beta \in]Z'[$ such that

$$G(\alpha_1, \alpha_2, \ldots, \alpha_m)(s) = \alpha(s) \quad \text{for all } s > t.$$

We now can use the method of the proof of Claim 1 to show that some variable of $F \circ G$ has the $\mathcal{F}$-property with respect to $]Z'[$.

Evidently, $G \circ F$ is almost constant and it preserves $]Z'[$ by Lemma 4.4. and Lemma 4.6..

Since G is almost constant, we have $\varphi^s_G = \varphi^s_{\times G}$ for $s > t$ where t is a certain integer. Therefore $\times G$ is almost constant, too, and it preserves $]Z'[$.

<u>Claim 5</u>. If $Z' \subseteq Z_2$, $Z' =]Z'[$, and $\beta \notin Z'$, then

$$[U(Z') \cup \{C_\beta\}] = P_2.$$

Proof of claim 5. By the definition of $U(Z')$, for any $F \in P_2$, the function $T_{\beta,F}$ of Lemma 4.7. is contained in $U(Z')$. Therefore $F \in [U(Z') \cup \{C_\beta\}]$ which proves the claim.

For $i \geq 1$, we define the ω-word β_i by

$$\beta_i(t) = \begin{cases} 1 & \text{if } t = ki \text{ for some } k \in \mathbb{N} \\ 0 & \text{otherwise} \end{cases}$$

and put

$$\tilde{Z} = \{\beta_i : i \geq 1\}.$$

<u>Claim 6</u>. If $Z^{(1)} \subseteq \tilde{Z}$, $Z^{(2)} \subseteq \tilde{Z}$, then $Z^{(1)} \neq Z^{(2)}$ implies $]Z^{(1)}[\neq]Z^{(2)}[$.

Proof of claim 6. Without loss of generality we can suppose that there is an α such that $\alpha \in Z^{(1)}$, $\alpha \notin Z^{(2)}$. We now assume $]Z^{(1)}[=]Z^{(2)}[$. As $\alpha \in Z^{(1)}$, we have $\alpha \in]Z^{(1)}[$ and therefore $\alpha \in]Z^{(2)}[$. Hence there is a $\beta \in Z^{(2)}$ such that $\alpha \in]\beta[$ and thus $\alpha(s) = \beta(s)$ for $s \geq r$ for some r. Since

$$\alpha(t) = \begin{cases} 1 & \text{if } t = ki \text{ for some } k \in \mathbb{N} \\ 0 & \text{otherwise,} \end{cases}$$

$$\beta(t) = \begin{cases} 1 & \text{if } t = kj \text{ for some } k \in \mathbb{N} \\ 0 & \text{otherwise} \end{cases}$$

for some fixed integers i and j, we obtain $i = j$ and hence $\alpha = \beta$. This contradicts $\alpha \notin Z^{(2)}$.

Now we are in a position to prove Theorem 4.15.. Let $Z^{(1)}$ and $Z^{(2)}$ be two nonempty subsets of $\tilde{Z}$ such that $Z^{(1)} \nsubseteq Z^{(2)}$ and $Z^{(2)} \nsubseteq Z^{(1)}$. By Claim 4, $\underline{U(Z^{(1)})}$ and $\underline{U(Z^{(2)})}$ are subalgebras. Further, for $i = 1,2$, $U(Z^{(i)}) \neq P_2$, $U(Z^{(1)}) \nsubseteq U(Z^{(2)})$, $U(Z^{(2)}) \nsubseteq U(Z^{(1)})$ by Claim 3 ii). By Lemma 1.5., $U(Z^{(i)})$ is contained in a certain maximal subalgebra $\underline{N_i}$ of $\underline{P_2}$, $i = 1,2$. Suppose $N_1 = N_2$. Obviously, there is a constant C_β with $C_\beta \notin U(Z^{(1)})$, $C_\beta \in U(Z^{(2)})$. Then, by Claim 5,

$$[U(Z^{(1)}) \cup \{C_\beta\}] = P_2$$

and

$$[U(Z^{(1)}) \cup \{C_\beta\}] \subseteq [U(Z^{(1)}) \cup U(Z^{(2)})] \subseteq N_1 \subset P_2.$$

This contradiction proves $N_1 \neq N_2$.
As the number of different subsets of $\tilde{Z}$ which do not contain each other pairwise is $\mathfrak{c}$, the number of maximal subalgebras of $\underline{P_2}$ is at least $\mathfrak{c}$. Since the number of sequential functions is countable, the power set of P_2 has the cardinality $\mathfrak{c}$, and therefore the number of maximal subalgebras is at most $\mathfrak{c}$.

By Lemma 1.7., we have the following version of Theorem 4.12..

> <u>Theorem 4.15.</u> There is a countable set $\mathfrak{M}$ of maximal subalgebras of $\underline{P_k}$ such that a finite subset M of P_k is complete if and only if $M \nsubseteq N$ holds for any $N \in \mathfrak{M}$.

Note that the proof of Lemma 1.7. gives no effective way to construct the set $\mathfrak{M}$.

4.3. The Undecidability of Completeness

The above results (especially Theorem 4.2.,Theorem 4.14.) show that there is no finite set $\mathfrak{N}$ of subalgebras of $\underline{P_k}$ such that a set $M \subseteq P_k$ is complete if and only if $M \nsubseteq N$ for any $N \in \mathfrak{N}$. Therefore the algebraic approach to the completeness problem is not effective. In this paragraph we shall improve this result. We prove that there is no effective way to solve the completeness problem.

Theorem 4.16. There is no algorithm which, for a given finite set contained in P_k, decides whether or not it is complete in $\underline{P_k}$.

Proof. In paragraph 1.2. we have noted that there is a normal Post algorithm $A = (X, \mu, \{(x,w_x) : x \in X\})$ such that it is undecidable whether or not a word $w \in X^+$ has a finite derivation. Without loss of generality let $X = \{3,4,\dots,k-1\}$, $k = |X| + 3$. We shall consider three special functions F_w, F_o, F_1 over E_k and prove that $\{F_w, F_o, F_1\}$ is complete if and only if w has a finite derivation. Then we have the undecidability of the completeness of $\{F_w, F_o, F_1\}$, and therefore the theorem is proved.

In order to give the definitions of F_w, F_o, F_1 we introduce some notations. An ω-word $\alpha = \alpha(1)\alpha(2)\dots$ is called a 1-word iff there are numbers $t_1(\alpha) \geq 0$, $t_2(\alpha) \geq 1$ such that

$$\alpha(1) = \alpha(2) = \dots = \alpha(t_1) = 2,$$

$$1 = \alpha(t_2) = \alpha(t_2+1) = \dots ,$$

$$\alpha(t_1+1), \alpha(t_1+2), \dots, \alpha(t_2-1) \in X.$$

An ω-word $\beta = \beta(1)\beta(2)\dots$ is called a 0-word if there is a number t such that

$$0 = \beta(t) = \beta(t+1) = \dots .$$

For a word $w \in X^*$ of length l we define the 1-word α_w by

$$t_1(\alpha_w) = 1, \quad t_2(\alpha_w) = l + 2,$$

$$\alpha(2)\alpha(3)\dots\alpha(l+1) = w .$$

We define the sequential function F_w by

$$F_w(\gamma) = \alpha_w$$

for all ω-words γ over E_k.

The function F_o has to model a derivation step of the normal Post algorithm A. The exact definition is given by the following conditions:

i) Let $\alpha(r) = 0$ for some $r \geq 1$. Then we put

$$F_o(\alpha)(s) = \alpha(s) \quad \text{for } s \geq r.$$

ii) Let α be a 1-word starting with t_1 times the letter 2, followed by the word $w' \in X^*$ of length u. If $u < \mu$, then $F_o(\alpha)$ has to be a 0-word. If $u \geq \mu$, then $F_o(\alpha)$ has to be a 1-word starting with $t_1 + \mu$ times the letter 2 and followed by the word w'' with $w' \Rightarrow w''$.

iii) If α is not a 1-word and there is no letter 0 in α, then $F_o(\alpha)$ has to be a 0-word.

We prove that F_o is a sequential function. We give an automaton inducing F_o. We put

$$\mathfrak{A} = (E_k, E_k, Z, g, f, z_o)$$

where

$$Z = \{z_o, z_o', z_o'', z'\} \cup \{[i]w_x z' : x \in X, 1 \le i \le \mu-1\} \cup \{pz' : qp = w_x \text{ for some } q \text{ and } x\},$$

$$g(z,0) = z_o', \quad f(z,0) = 0 \quad \text{for } z \in Z,$$

$$g(z_o',x) = z_o', \quad f(z_o',x) = x \quad \text{for } x \in E_k,$$

$$g(z_o,x) = \begin{cases} z_o'' & \text{if } x = 1 \\ z_o & \text{if } x = 2 \\ [\mu-1]w_x z' & \text{if } x \in X, \end{cases}$$

$$f(z_o,x) = \begin{cases} 0 & \text{if } x = 1 \\ 2 & \text{if } x = 2 \\ 2 & \text{if } x \in X, \end{cases}$$

$$g(z_o'',x) = z_o'', \quad f(z_o'',x) = 0 \quad \text{for } x \in E_k \setminus \{0\},$$

$$g([i]w_y z',x) = \begin{cases} [i-1]w_y z' & \text{if } i > 1,\ x \in X \\ w_y z' & \text{if } i = 1,\ x \in X \\ z_o'' & \text{if } x \in \{1,2\}, \end{cases}$$

$$f([i]w_y z',x) = \begin{cases} 2 & \text{if } x \in X \\ 0 & \text{if } x \notin X, \end{cases}$$

$$g(ypz',x) = \begin{cases} z_o'' & \text{if } x \ge 2, \\ pz' & \text{if } x = 1, \end{cases} \qquad f(ypz',x) = \begin{cases} 0 & \text{if } x \ge 2 \\ y & \text{if } x = 1, \end{cases}$$

$$g(z',x) = \begin{cases} z' & \text{if } x = 1 \\ z_o'' & \text{if } x \ge 2, \end{cases} \qquad f(z',x) = \begin{cases} 1 & \text{if } x = 1 \\ 0 & \text{if } x \ge 2. \end{cases}$$

It is easy to see that $F_{\mathfrak{A}} = F_o$.

We now define the function $F_1 \in P_k^{\,3}$ by the following conditions:

i) If $\alpha_3(r) = 0$ for some r, then

$$F_1(\alpha_1, \alpha_2, \alpha_3)(s) = \alpha_3(s) \quad \text{for } s \geq r.$$

ii) If α_3 is a 1-word such that $\alpha_3 = 2^u w'11\ldots$ with $l(w') \geq \mu$, then $F_1(\alpha_1, \alpha_2, \alpha_3)$ is a 0-word.

iii) If α_3 does not have the structure given in i) or ii), then

$$F_1(\alpha_1, \alpha_2, \alpha_3) = G(\alpha_1, \alpha_2)$$

where G is a function with $G \in P_k^{\,2}$ and $[\{G\}] = P_k$ (see Theorem 4.3.).

It is left to the reader to prove that F_1 is sequential.
By (F_w), (F_o), (F_1) we denote logical nets inducing F_w, F_o, F_1, respectively.

Claim 1. If w has a finite derivation, then $\{F_w, F_o, F_1\}$ is complete in P_k.

Proof of claim 1. Let $w = w_o \Rightarrow w_1 \Rightarrow w_2 \Rightarrow \ldots \Rightarrow w_{n-1} \Rightarrow w_n$ be the finite derivation of w. Then $l(w_n) < \mu$. The sequential function F' induced by the net of Figure 17 satisfies

$$F'(\alpha) = 2^{\mu n+1} w_n 111\ldots$$

and hence F'' defined by

$$F''(\alpha_1, \alpha_2) = F_1(\alpha_1, \alpha_2, F'(\alpha_1))$$

coincides with G. Thus

$$[\{F_w, F_o, F_1\}] \supseteq [\{G\}] = P_k.$$

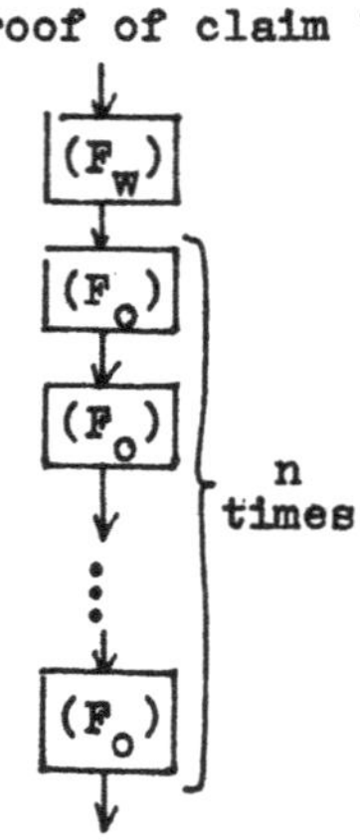

Figure 17

Let F be a sequential function of $[\{F_w, F_o, F_1\}]$. Then there exists a logical net N such that $F_N = F$ and N is constructed by the elementary operations from (F_w), (F_o), (F_1). With N we associated the inductively defined sequence $V = (V_1, V_2, \ldots)$ of logical nets contained in $\{(F_w), (F_o), (F_1)\}$:

i) V_1 is the last elementary net of N, i.e. V_1 is contained in $\{(F_w), (F_o), (F_1)\}$ and the output line of V_1 is the output line of N.

Let $V_1, V_2, \ldots, V_r$ be defined.

ii) If $V_r = (F_w)$, then V is finite and $V = (V_1, V_2, \ldots, V_r)$.

iii) If $V_r = (F_o)$ and the input line of V_r is also an input line of N, then V is finite and $V = (V_1, V_2, \ldots, V_r)$.
If $V_r = (F_o)$ and the input line of V_r is not an input line of N, then the input line of V_r is the output line of some $V' \in \{(F_w), (F_o), (F_1)\}$. Then we put $V_{r+1} = V'$.

iv) Let $V_r = (F_1)$. If the third input line of V_r is also an input line of N, then $V = (V_1, V_2, \ldots, V_r)$. In the opposite case, the third input line of V_r is the output line of a certain $V' \in \{(F_w), (F_o), (F_1)\}$. Then we put $V_{r+1} = V'$.

By definition, V is finite or a periodic sequence (the second case can only appear if feedback is used in the construction of N). We prove that V is finite for all N which can be constructed from (F_w), (F_o), (F_1). If the sequence V contains (F_w), then it is finite by definition ii). Let therefore V consist only of nets (F_o) and (F_1). We consider the subnet N_i of N which contains $V_1, V_2, \ldots, V_i$ and the edges between the V_j's, $1 \leq j \leq i$, and the input lines of N_i are the input lines of the nets V_l, $1 \leq l \leq i$, which are not connected with a net V_m, $1 \leq m \leq i$. Let $x(t)$ be the signal which is emitted at the moment t by the source on the input line of V_i if $V_i = (F_o)$, or on the third input line of V_i if $V_i = (F_1)$. If $x(1) = 0$, then the output of N_i coincides with $x(t)$ by i) of the definition of F_o and F_1. Therefore F_{N_i} does not depend delayed on the corresponding variable, and thus we cannot apply the feedback operation. This implies the finiteness of V.

<u>Claim 2</u>. If $\{F_w, F_o, F_1\}$ is complete, then w has a finite derivation.

Proof of claim 2. Assume that w has an infinite derivation. Since $\{F_w, F_o, F_1\}$ is complete, we can construct a net N from (F_w), (F_o), and (F_1) such that $F_N = G$. We consider the associated finite sequence $(V_1, V_2, \ldots, V_r)$. Obviously, $V_r = (F_w)$ because, in the opposite case, we have $F_N(0,0) = 0$ (by i) of the definition of F_o and F_1), which contradicts $F_N = G$. Further, there has to be a number $s < r$ such that $V_s = (F_1)$, since N induces a constant mapping in the opposite case. Without loss of generality we suppose that

$$V_{s+1} = V_{s+2} = \ldots = V_{r-1} = (F_o).$$

We regard the nets N_1 and N_2 of Figure 18 and their induced functions F_3 and F_4.

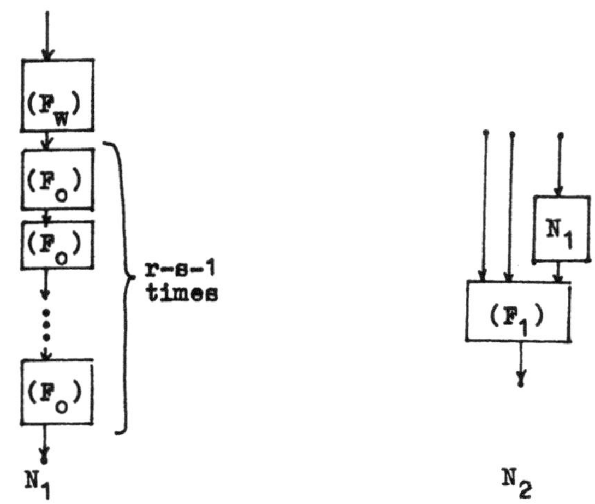

Figure 18

For these functions we have

$$F_3(\alpha) = 2^{\mu(r-s-1)+1}w'111\ldots$$

where w' is the word derived from w in $r-s-1$ steps, and

$$F_4(\alpha_1, \alpha_2, \alpha_3) = \beta_1 \beta_2 \ldots \beta_{\mu(r-s-1)+1} \gamma_1 \gamma_2 \ldots \gamma_{\mu-1} 000\ldots$$

where $\beta_1, \beta_2, \ldots, \beta_{\mu(r-s-1)+1}, \gamma_1, \gamma_2, \ldots, \gamma_{\mu-1} \in E_k$ since $l(w') \geq \mu$ by assumption. Therefore we obtain that $F_N(\alpha_1, \alpha_2)$ is a 0-word for all α_1, α_2. Again, this contradicts $F_N = G$.

Combining Claim 1 and Claim 2 we conclude that $\{F_w, F_o, F_1\}$ is complete if and only if w has a finite derivation. Because the finiteness of the derivation of a word is undecidable, the completeness of a finite subset of P_k is undecidable, too.

The above observations prove Theorem 4.16. only for a certain k. We code the elements of E_k by words of length $]\log_2 k[$ and modify the definitions of a 0-word, 1-word, F_w, F_o, F_1 slightly and can give an analogous proof for E_2 considering words of length $i \cdot]\log_2 k[$. This implies that Theorem 4.16. is valid for all $k \geq 2$.

Without proof we add two consequences of Theorem 4.16..

<u>Theorem 4.17.</u> It is undecidable whether or not a sequential function generates P_k.

<u>Theorem 4.18.</u> It is undecidable whether or not $F \in [M]$ holds for a given constant sequential function and a given subset M of P_k.

Exercises

1. Show that, for any $n \geq 1$, there is a basis of $M_{T_0} \subseteq P_2$ which consists of exactly n elements (cf. /Da4/).
2. Determine $[\{F_{(id;1;0)}\}]_s$.
3. Prove that the set of all almost constant functions of P_k forms a subalgebra of $\underline{P_k}$.
4. Let J be the set of functions induced by automata which satisfy the condition $g(z_0,p) = \begin{cases} z_0 & \text{if } l(p) \text{ is even} \\ z_1 & \text{if } l(p) \text{ is odd} \end{cases}$. Prove that $\underline{J}$ is a subalgebra of $\underline{P_k}$ which can be generated by a single function.
5. Prove Lemma 4.7. for $k \geq 3$.
6. Show that F_1 of the proof of Theorem 4.16. is sequential.
7. i) Prove the existence of a sequential function $F \in P_k^{\,2}$, $k \geq 2$, which depends essentially on both variables such that $[P_k^{\,1} \cup \{F\}]$ is not complete in P_k.
   ii) Let $k \geq 3$ and $F_{(f)} \in P_k^{\,2}$ depend essentially on both variables. Show that $[P_k^{\,1} \cup \{F_{(f)}\}] = P_k$.
8. i) Let $[M] \supseteq M_{\{id\}}$. Prove that M is complete if and only if $\varphi(M) = \{\varphi_F^1 : F \in M\}$ is not contained in any maximal subalgebra of P_k'.
   ii) Show that it is undecidable whether or not $[M] \supseteq M_{\{id\}}$ holds for a finite set $M \subseteq P_k$ (cf. /Da11/).

5. MODIFICATIONS OF THE COMPLETENESS PROBLEM

Regarding the negative result in paragraph 4.3. we are interested in modifications of the completeness problem. The following two approaches can be considered:

- We do not require that all functions of P_k can be generated by the sequential functions of M. With any function F we associate a subset $M(F)$ of P_k, which contains functions which are nearly related to F in a certain sense, and we require that, for any function F, the subalgebra generated by M contains at least one element of $M(F)$. In the paragraphs 5.1 - 5.3. we shall give three such modifications.
- We do not consider an arbitrary set M; we regard only subsets of P_k which satisfy additional properties. For instance, let M contain all functions of a certain subset of P_k or let M contain only sequential functions with certain special properties. Such approaches will be considered in the paragraphs 5.4., 5.5.

5.1. Metric Completeness

We consider a metric in the set $P_k{}^n$ and modify the completeness as follows: with F we associate a neighbourhood with respect to the metric and require that, for any F, we can generate an element of the neighbourhood of F, where the neighbourhood can be arbitrarily small.

The distance $d(F,G)$ of two sequential functions F and G is defined as follows:

$$d(F,G) = \frac{1}{n} \text{ if and only if } \varphi_F^i = \varphi_G^i \text{ for } i < n \text{ and } \varphi_F^n \neq \varphi_G^n.$$

It is easy to prove that d is a metric in P_k (it is known as Baire metric).

$M \subseteq P_k$ is called metrically complete (m-complete) if and only if, for any $\varepsilon > 0$ and any $F \in P_k$, there is a function $G \in [M]$ such that $d(F,G) < \varepsilon$.

In the sequel we shall use an equivalent approach, too. Let $t \geq 1$. We say that two functions G and F are t-equivalent if and only if $\varphi_F^i = \varphi_G^i$ for $i \leq t$. Obviously, G and F are t-equivalent if and only if $d(F,G) \leq \frac{1}{t}$. $M_1, M_2 \subseteq P_k$ are called t-equivalent iff, for any function $F \in M_1$, there is a function $G \in M_2$ which is t-equiva-

lent to F, and conversely, for any function $G' \in M_2$, there is a function $F' \in M_1$ which is t-equivalent to G'.
M_1 and M_2 are called metrically equivalent (m-equivalent) if and only if they are t-equivalent for any $t > 0$. Evidently, $M \subseteq P_k$ is m-complete if and only if $[M]$ is m-equivalent to P_k.
We illustrate the m-completeness by some examples which also prove that the m-completeness is a properly weaker concept than the usual completeness.

Example 5.1. Clearly, P_k is m-equivalent to P_k; therefore any complete set is also m-complete.

Example 5.2. For any function $F \in P_k$ and any $t \geq 1$, we define $F^{(t)}$ by

$$\varphi^{i}_{F^{(t)}} = \begin{cases} \varphi^{i}_{F} & \text{if } i \leq t \\ k_0 & \text{if } i > t. \end{cases}$$

Obviously, F and $F^{(t)}$ are t-equivalent. Therefore the set

$$M^{(t)} = \{F^{(t)} : F \in P_k\}$$

is t-equivalent to P_k. We put

$$M = \bigcup_{t \geq 1} M^{(t)}.$$

It is easy to prove that $\underline{M}$ is a subalgebra of $\underline{P_k}$. Further, M is m-equivalent to P_k. However, M is not complete since M does not contain $F_{(id)}$.
We note that there are infinitely many different subalgebras of $\underline{P_k}$ which are m-equivalent to P_k. We have to use only other periods beginning at the t-th moment.

Now we give some results which show the difference between completeness and m-completeness. By Lemma 1.2., any complete set of P_k contains a finite complete subset. Subalgebras which are m-equivalent to the set P_k have a different behaviour.

Theorem 5.1. i) There is a subalgebra which is m-equivalent to P_k and has a finite basis.
ii) There is a subalgebra which is m-equivalent to P_k, has no finite system of generators, and has a system of generators which contains no basis.
iii) There is a subalgebra which is m-equivalent to P_k and has an infinite basis.

Proof. i) Take P_k.
ii) We consider the set M of Example 5.2.. If $\{F_1, F_2, \ldots, F_s\}$ is a finite set, then there is a number r such that

$$\{F_1, F_2, \ldots, F_s\} \subseteq M^{(r)}.$$

Hence

$$[\{F_1, F_2, \ldots, F_s\}] \subseteq M^{(r)}.$$

Since $M^{(r)} \neq M$, we obtain that $\underline{M}$ has no finite system of generators.
Let F_t be the function of $M^{(t)}$ which is t-equivalent to a function F with $[\{F\}] = P_k$ (see Theorem 4.3.). Then $\{F_1, F_2, \ldots\}$ is a system of generators for $\underline{M}$. However, $i < j$ implies $F_i \in [\{F_j\}] = M^{(j)}$. Since any system of generators for $\underline{M}$ is infinite, any subset of $\{F_1, F_2, \ldots\}$ which generates M is infinite. Hence such a set contains at least two different function, and thus it is reducible.
Note that this also proves that any subset of $\{F_1, F_2, \ldots\}$ that is m-complete is reducible.
iii) Let β_i be the ω-word with

$$\beta_i(s) = \begin{cases} 1 & \text{if } s = k \cdot i \text{ for some } k \in \mathbb{N} \\ 0 & \text{otherwise.} \end{cases}$$

For $F \in P_k$, we define F_{β_i} by

$$\varphi^j_{F_{\beta_i}} = \begin{cases} \varphi^j_F & \text{if } j \leq i \\ k_{\beta_i(j)} & \text{if } j > i. \end{cases}$$

Then we put

$$M_{\beta_t} = \{F_{\beta_t} : F \in P_k\} \quad \text{and} \quad M_1 = \bigcup_{t \geq 1} M_{\beta_t}.$$

Then M_1 forms a subalgebra and is m-equivalent to P_k. We prove that M_1 has a basis. Let $G_t \in M_{\beta_t}$ be a function which is t-equivalent to a generator of P_k. Then $\{G_1, G_2, \ldots\}$ is a system of generators for M_1. Since

$$\alpha(F_{\beta_j}) = (\alpha F)_{\beta_j} \quad \text{for} \quad \alpha \in \{\zeta, \tau, \Delta, \nabla\},$$

$$(F \circ G)_{\beta_j} = F_{\beta_j} \circ G, \quad \text{and} \quad \times F_{\beta_j} \in M_{\beta_j},$$

we obtain that any function $G \in [\{G_1, G_2, \ldots, G_{i-1}, G_{i+1}, G_{i+2}, \ldots\}]$ satisfies $G \in M_{\beta_j}$ for some $j \neq i$. Therefore

$$G_i \notin [\{G_1, G_2, \ldots, G_{i-1}, G_{i+1}, G_{i+2}, \ldots\}].$$

Hence $\{G_1, G_2, \ldots\}$ is a basis for $\underline{M}_1$.

The feedback operation is of great importance in $\underline{P_k}$ (see paragraph 4.1.), however, concerning the m-completeness the other operations are sufficient. More precisely, we have

Theorem 5.2. $[M]$ and $[M]_s$ are m-equivalent.

Proof. We show that $\times F$ and $\underbrace{F \circ (F \circ (F \ldots (F \circ (F}_{t-1 \text{ times}} \circ \Delta F)) \ldots))$

are t-equivalent. We use induction on t.

Since F depends delayed on its first variable, we have $\varphi^1_{\times F} = \varphi^1_{\Delta F}$.

Thus $\times F$ and ΔF are 1-equivalent.

By induction hypothesis, $\times F$ and $\underbrace{F \circ (F \circ \ldots (F}_{t-2 \text{ times}} \circ \Delta F) \ldots)$ are (t-1)-equivalent. By Lemma 2.8., we have $\times F = F \circ \times F$. Since F depends delayed on the first variable, we obtain that $\times F$ and $\underbrace{F \circ (F \circ \ldots (F}_{t-1 \text{ times}} \circ \Delta F) \ldots)$ are t-equivalent.

A subalgebra $\underline{M}$ is called t-precomplete, $t > 0$, if and only if M is not t-equivalent to P_k and, for each $F \notin M$, $[M \cup \{F\}]$ is t-equivalent to P_k.

A subalgebra $\underline{M}$ is called m-precomplete if and only if M is not m-equivalent to P_k and, for any $F \notin M$, $[M \cup \{F\}]$ is m-equivalent to P_k.

Theorem 5.3. i) M is m-complete if and only if M is not contained in any m-precomplete subalgebra.

ii) The cardinality of the set of all m-precomplete subalgebras is $\aleph_0$.

Proof. The proof will be given in some steps.

Claim 1. Let $t \geq 1$, and let $M_0 \subset M_1 \subset M_2 \subset \ldots \subset M_n \subset \ldots$ be an infinite chain of subalgebras. If $\bigcup_{i \geq 0} M_i$ is a subalgebra t-equivalent to P_k, then there is a number s such that M_j is t-equivalent to P_k for $j \geq s$.

Proof of claim 1. Since $\bigcup_{i \geq 0} M_i$ is t-equivalent to P_k, there are functions F_1, F_2 such that F_1 is t-equivalent to $F_{(sh)}$ and F_2 is t-equivalent to $F_{(id;1;0)}$. Hence there is a number s such that $F_1, F_2 \in M_s$, and thus $[\{F_1, F_2\}] \subseteq M_s$. As $[\{F_1, F_2\}]$ is t-equivalent to P_k, $M_s, M_{s+1}, \ldots$ are also t-equivalent to P_k.

Claim 2. Any subalgebra M that is not t-equivalent to P_k is contained in a t-precomplete subalgebra of $\underline{P_k}$.

Proof of claim 2. Use Claim 1 and the method of the proof of Lemma 1.5.

Claim 3. For any $t > 0$, the number of t-precomplete subalgebras of P_k is finite.

Proof of claim 3. For a subalgebra $\underline{M'}$, we define $M_{(t)} = M' \cap M^{(t)}$ (see Example 5.2.). Clearly, $M_{(t)}$ forms a subalgebra. Let

$$W = \{F : F \in M^{(t)},\ F \in P_k{}^2 \cup P_k{}^1 \cup P_k{}^0\}.$$

Evidently, W is a finite set.
We say that a function F has the U-property, $U \subseteq P_k$, if, for all functions $G_1, G_2, \ldots, G_n \in U$, the function H defined by

$$H(p_1, p_2) = F(G_1(p_{11}, p_{12}, \ldots, p_{1r_1}), \ldots, G_n(p_{n1}, p_{n2}, \ldots, p_{nr_n})),$$
$$p_{ij} \in \{p_1, p_2\} \text{ for } 1 \leq i \leq n,\ 1 \leq j \leq r_i,$$

satisfies the condition

$$\varphi_H^i = \varphi_{F'}^i, \quad \text{for } i \leq t \text{ and some } F' \in U.$$

Now, let S be the set of those subsets $U \subseteq W$ such that any function $F \in U$ has the U-property and U is not t-equivalent to P_k. For $U \in S$ we define U' as the set of all functions of P_k that have the U-property. Let $S' = \{U' : U \in S\}$. Obviously, S' is finite. It is easy to prove that, for $U' \in S'$, $\underline{U'}$ is a subalgebra and U' is not t-equivalent to P_k.
Let $\underline{M'}$ be a subalgebra of $\underline{P_k}$ which is not t-equivalent to P_k. Then $M_{(t)} \cap P_k{}^2$ has the $(M_{(t)} \cap P_k{}^2)$-property. Therefore $M_{(t)} \cap P_k{}^2$ is an element of S. Further, each function of M' has the $(M_{(t)} \cap P_k{}^2)$-property. Thus M' is contained in some element of S'. (Notice that it is possible that a certain element of S' is not t-precomplete for all $t > 0$.)

Claim 4. Let $t>0$. If M is a t-precomplete subalgebra, then M contains all functions F with

$$\varphi^i_F(x_1(1),\ldots,x_n(1),\ldots,x_1(i),\ldots,x_n(i)) = x_j(i) \quad \text{for} \quad i \leq t.$$

This can be proved like Lemma 4.13..

Claim 5. For each $t>0$, any t-precomplete subalgebra is m-precomplete.

Proof of claim 5. By Claim 4 the sequential functions F_1, F_2, F_3 given by the following conditions are in the t-precomplete subalgebra $\underline{M}$:

$$\varphi^i_{F_1}(x_1(1),x_2(1),\ldots,x_1(i),x_2(i)) = \begin{cases} x_1(i) & \text{for} \quad i \leq t \\ sh(x_1(i),x_2(i)) & \text{for} \quad i>t, \end{cases}$$

$$\varphi^i_{F_2}(x(1),\ldots,x(i)) = \begin{cases} x(i) & \text{for} \quad i \leq t \\ x(i-1) & \text{for} \quad i>t, \end{cases}$$

$$\varphi^i_{F_3}(x_1(1),x_2(1),\ldots,x_1(i),x_2(i)) = \begin{cases} x_1(i) & \text{for} \quad i \leq t \\ x_2(i) & \text{for} \quad i>t. \end{cases}$$

Further, for each function $F \notin M$, $[M \cup \{F\}]$ is t-equivalent to P_k. Therefore $[M \cup \{F\}]$ contains functions G_1, G_2 such that

$$\varphi^i_{G_1}(x_1(1),x_2(1),\ldots,x_1(i),x_2(i)) = sh(x_1(i),x_2(i)) \quad \text{for} \quad i \leq t,$$

$$\varphi^i_{G_2}(x(1),x(2),\ldots,x(i)) = \begin{cases} k_0 & \text{for} \quad i=1 \\ x(i-1) & \text{for} \quad i \in \{2,3,\ldots,t\}. \end{cases}$$

Then the functions H_1, H_2 defined by

$$H_1(p_1,p_2) = F_3(G_1(p_1,p_2),F_1(p_1,p_2)),$$

$$H_2(p) = F_3(G_2(p),F_2(p))$$

coincide with $F_{(sh)}$ and $F_{(id;1;0)}$, respectively. Therefore $[M \cup \{F\}] = P_k$, especially $[M \cup \{F\}]$ is m-equivalent to P_k. Hence M is m-precomplete.

Claim 6. Any m-precomplete subalgebra is t-precomplete for some t.

Proof of Claim 6. Let $\underline{M}$ be m-precomplete. Then there is a number t such that M is not t-equivalent to P_k. By Claim 2, M is contained in a certain t-precomplete subalgebra N. If $M \neq N$, then M is not m-precomplete. Therefore $M = N$.

We now prove the theorem. Let M be contained in an m-precomplete subalgebra N of P_k. Then $[M] \subseteq N$, and therefore M is not m-complete.
Let M be not m-complete. Then $[M]$ is not m-equivalent to P_k, i.e. there is a number t such that $[M]$ is not t-equivalent to P_k. By Claim 2, $[M]$ is contained in a t-precomplete subalgebra $\underline{N}$ of $\underline{P_k}$, and $\underline{N}$ is also m-precomplete by Claim 5. This proves i).
ii) follows from Claim 3, 5, 6.

We notice that any m-precomplete subalgebra of $\underline{P_k}$ is also a maximal subalgebra of $\underline{P_k}$ by the proof of Claim 3. Regarding Theorem 4.14. we obtain that "almost all" maximal subalgebras of $\underline{P_k}$ are already m-equivalent to P_k. Although we have made an important progress in reducing the number of the subalgebras in the algebraic completeness criterion (Theorem 4.14, Theorem 4.15, and Theorem 5.3.) this criterion is not effective by Theorem 5.3.ii). Concerning the decidability of m-completeness we have

Theorem 5.4. The m-completeness of a finite subset of P_k is undecidable.

Proof. The proof follows the same line as that of Theorem 4.16.. We have to modify F_1 sligthly. We refer the reader to /Bu3/ and /KAP/ for details.

Let $t > 0$. $M \subseteq P_k$ is called t-complete if and only if $[M]$ is t-equivalent to P_k.
Obviously the t-completeness is a properly weaker concept than metric completeness (consider $M^{(t)}$). By practical reasons it is of interest, because, for each real automaton, there is an upper bound for the run time in practice. Thus we have to consider only the behaviour of the automaton on words of bounded length.

Theorem 5.5. It is decidable whether or not a given finite subset of P_k is t-complete.

Proof. It is sufficient to consider the sequences $(\varphi_F^1, \varphi_F^2, \ldots, \varphi_F^t)$ of length t associated with $F \in P_k$. Since there is only a finite number of such sequences associated with functions of $P_k{}^2$ and there is a function $G \in P_k{}^2$ with $[\{G\}] = P_k$, we can apply the same algorithm as in the proof of Theorem 3.2..

Again, we have the completeness criterion that M is t-complete if and only if it is not contained in any t-precomplete subalgebra. By

Claim 3 of the proof of Theorem 5.3., we know that the number of t-precomplete subalgebras is finite, and we have some information on the structure of these subalgebras. An effective description of t-precomplete subalgebras is given in /Bu5/. We omit the description because it is very long and its proof takes nearly 200 pages. By Claim 5 and Claim 6 of Theorem 5.3., we also have an effective description of the m-precomplete subalgebras.

5.2. Kleene-Completeness

Nowadays an automaton is often used as an acceptor for input words. With respect to completeness, for any acceptable set R, we have to generate from M an automaton which accepts R. Usually, in the theory of automata, the states are used to accept words. As the sequential function do not reflect the inner structure of the automaton or the logical net, we have to use outputs as accepting sets. It is known that both concepts of acceptance have the same acceptance power (see /St/, I, §5).

We say that the sequential function $F : X^{*} \to Y^{*}$ accepts the word $p = a_1 a_2 \dots a_n \in X^{+}$ by the set Y', $\emptyset \subsetneq Y' \subsetneq Y$, if and only if

$$\varphi_F^n(a_1, a_2, \dots, a_n) \in Y'.$$

Let $R \subseteq X^{+}$. We say that R is accepted by the sequential function $F : X^{*} \to Y^{*}$ and the set Y', $\emptyset \subsetneq Y' \subsetneq Y$, if and only if it holds that F accepts $p \in X^{+}$ by Y' if and only if $p \in R$.
In the sequel we shall say that F accepts R if there is a set Y' such that F accepts R by Y'.
The next theorem characterizes the acceptable sets.

Theorem 5.6. The following statements are equivalent:
i) R is accepted by some sequential function.
ii) R is regular (see paragraph 1.2.).

For a proof we refer to /St/, /GP/, /CEW/.

Example 5.3. Let $F \in P_3^{\,2}$ be defined by

$$\varphi_F^1 = k_0, \qquad \varphi_F^{2n} = k_0 \quad \text{for } n \geq 1,$$

$$\varphi_F^{2n+1}(x_1(1), x_2(1), \dots, x_1(2n+1), x_2(2n+1)) = x_1(2n+1) \quad \text{for } n \geq 1.$$

Then F accepts

$$R_0 = \{p : p \in (E_3{}^2)^*, \ l(p) = 1 \ \text{ or } \ l(p) \text{ is even}\} \\ \cup \{p(0,x) : x \in E_3, \ p \in (E_3{}^2)^*, \ l(p) \geq 2, \ l(p) \text{ is even}\}$$

by $Y' = \{0\}$, and it accepts

$$R_1 = \{p(1,x) : x \in E_3, \ p \in (E_3{}^2)^*, \ l(p) \geq 2, \ l(p) \text{ is even}\}$$

by $Y' = \{1\}$. We define G_i, $i \geq 1$, by

$$\varphi^j_{G_i} = \varphi^j_F \quad \text{for } j \neq 2i, \quad \varphi^{2i}_{G_i} = k_2.$$

For any $i \geq 1$, G_i accepts also R_1 by $\{1\}$.

$M \subseteq P_k$ is called a Kleene-set in P_k iff

i) $\underline{M}$ is a subalgebra of $\underline{P_k}$, and

ii) for each n and each regular set $R \subseteq (E_k{}^n)^+$ there is a sequential function $F \in M$ such that F accepts R.

M is called Kleene-complete iff $[M]$ is a Kleene-set in P_k.

If $k = 2$, then there are exactly two functions F_1 and F_2 which accept a given regular set. For these functions,

$$F_1 = F_{(non)} \circ F_2 \quad \text{and} \quad F_2 = F_{(non)} \circ F_1.$$

Conversely, F_1 and F_2 satisfying these relations accept the same regular sets. Therefore the relation $\sim$ given by

$F \sim G$ if and only if F and G accept the same sets

is an equivalence relation. Thus the Kleene-completeness in P_2 is a special case of completeness up to equivalence in the sense of /Sa/ and /BBK/.

<u>Example 5.4.</u> By the Theorem of Kleene, P_k is a Kleene-set.

<u>Example 5.5.</u> M_{T_i} is a Kleene-set in P_k for $i = 0,1,\dots,k-1$.

<u>Proof</u>. By Example 2.9., $\underline{M_{T_i}}$ is a subalgebra of $\underline{P_k}$. Let $R \subseteq (E_k{}^n)^+$ be a regular set. By the Theorem of Kleene (Theorem 5.6.), there are a sequential function F and a subset Y of E_k such that F accepts R by Y. If $\varphi^1_F \in T_i$, we have $F \in M_{T_i}$, and we have finished. Let $\varphi^1_F \notin T_i$.

Case 1. $(i,i,\dots,i) \in R$. Then $F((i,i,\dots,i)) = a \in Y$ and $a \neq i$. If $i \in Y$, too, we put $Y' = Y$. If $i \notin Y$, we put $Y' = (Y \setminus \{a\}) \cup \{i\}$.

Further let π be the permutation defined by

$$\pi(x) = \begin{cases} x & \text{for } x \neq a,\ x \neq i \\ a & \text{for } x = i, \\ i & \text{for } x = a. \end{cases}$$

Let F_1 denote the sequential function given by $F_1 = F_{(\pi)} \circ F$. Then F_1 is contained in M_{T_i}, and it accepts R by Y'.

Case 2. $(i,i,\dots,i) \notin R$. We choose

$$Y' = \begin{cases} (Y \setminus \{i\}) \cup \{a\} & \text{if } i \in Y \\ Y & \text{if } i \notin Y. \end{cases}$$

Then $F_1 \in M_{T_i}$ holds again, and F_1 accepts R by Y'.

Thus, any regular subset of $(E_k{}^n)^*$, $n \geq 1$, can be accepted by elements of M_{T_i}.

Note that M_{T_i} is not t-complete for $t > 0$, and thus M_{T_i} is not m-complete, because there is no function in M_{T_i} which is t-equivalent, $t > 0$, to the function $F_{(k_j)}$ with $j \neq i$. Therefore the concepts of m-completeness, t-completeness, $t > 0$, and Kleene-completeness are different, and clearly, the Kleene-completeness is properly weaker than the completeness.

Example 5.6. Let $k \geq 3$ and $Q \subseteq E_k$ with $|Q| \geq 2$. Let N_Q be the set of all sequential functions whose range is contained in Q^*. Then N_Q is a Kleene-set.

Proof. Obviously, N_Q is a subalgebra. Let S be a regular set, and let $F \in P_k$ be a sequential function which accepts S by $Y \subset E_k$. Let $f \in P_k'^{1}$ be the function with

$$f(x) = \begin{cases} a & \text{for } x \in Y \\ b & \text{otherwise} \end{cases}$$

where $\{a,b\} \subseteq Q$, $a \neq b$. Then $F_{(f)} \circ F \in N_Q$, and this function accepts S by $\{a\}$.

Lemma 5.7. Let M be a Kleene-set in P_2. Then

$$M \supseteq [\tilde{T}_0 \cup \{F_{(id;1;0)}, F_{(non;1;0)}\}]$$

or

$$M \supseteq [\tilde{T}_1 \cup \{F_{(id;1;1)}, F_{(non;1;1)}\}].$$

Proof. First we prove $M \supseteq \tilde{T}_0$ or $M \supseteq \tilde{T}_1$. Since $\widetilde{\underline{P_2}}$ is a subalgebra of $\underline{P_2}$, $M' = M \cap \widetilde{P_2}$ also forms a subalgebra.

i) M' contains a function F such that $F \notin \tilde{L}$.
We consider the regular set $(E_2{}^2)^* Q$ where $Q = \{(1,1)\}$. This set is accepted by $F_{(et)}$ and $F_{(sh)}$. In both cases $F \notin \tilde{L}$.

ii) There is a function F in M' with $F \notin \tilde{\mathcal{M}}$.
We consider $(E_2{}^2)^* Q$ with $Q = \{(0,1)\}$. The associated accepting functions are $F_{(f_1)}$ and $F_{(f_2)}$ where

$$f_1(x_1,x_2) = \begin{cases} 1 & \text{if } (x_1,x_2) = (0,1) \\ 0 & \text{otherwise} \end{cases}, \quad f_2 = \text{non} \circ f_1.$$

Obviously, $F_{(f_1)}, F_{(f_2)} \notin \tilde{\mathcal{M}}$.

iii) M' contains a function F which is not in $\tilde{S}$.
The proof can be given in an analogous way using $Q = \{(0,0), (1,1)\}$.
By Lemma 3.5., we have $M' = \widetilde{P_2}$ or $M' = \tilde{T}_i$ for some $i \in \{0,1\}$.

iv) There is a function $F \in M'$ such that $F \notin \tilde{T}_0 \cap \tilde{T}_1$.
We use the same Q as in iii) and can give an analogous proof.

Again, in the same way we obtain
v) M' contains functions F_1 and F_2 such that $F_1 \notin \widetilde{S(2)}$ and $F_2 \notin \widetilde{S'(2)}$ (the definition of $S(2)$ is given in exercise 3 of Chapter 3, $S'(2)$ denotes the set of all 1-separating functions of degree 2).

By the results of /JGK/ (see also exercise 8 of Chapter 2), $\tilde{T}_0$ has the following four maximal subalgebras

$$\tilde{T}_0 \cap \tilde{T}_1,\ \tilde{T}_0 \cap \tilde{L},\ \tilde{T}_0 \cap \tilde{\mathcal{M}},\ \widetilde{S(2)},$$

and the maximal subalgebras of $\tilde{T}_1$ are

$$\tilde{T}_0 \cap \tilde{T}_1,\ \tilde{T}_1 \cap \tilde{L},\ \tilde{T}_1 \cap \tilde{\mathcal{M}},\ \widetilde{S'(2)}.$$

If $M' \subsetneq \tilde{T}_i$ for some $i \in \{0,1\}$, then M' is contained in a certain maximal subalgebra of $\tilde{T}_i$. By i), ii), iv), and v), this is impossible. Therefore $M' \supseteq \tilde{T}_0$ or $M' \supseteq \tilde{T}_1$.

We consider

$$Q_1 = E_2^{*}\{1\}E_2 , \qquad Q_1' = E_2 \cup E_2^{*}\{0\}E_2 ,$$

$$Q_2 = E_2^{*}\{0\}E_2 , \qquad Q_2' = E_2 \cup E_2^{*}\{1\}E_2 .$$

Then the following table holds:

function	set accepted by $\{0\}$	set accepted by $\{1\}$
$F_{(id;1;0)}$	Q_1'	Q_1
$F_{(id;1;1)}$	Q_2	Q_2'
$F_{(non;1;0)}$	Q_2'	Q_2
$F_{(non;1;1)}$	Q_1	Q_1'

Since M is a Kleene-set, there are functions $F_1, F_2 \in M$ which accept Q_1 (and then Q_1', too) and Q_2 (and then Q_2', too), respectively. By the above table, we have

$$F_1 = F_{(id;1;0)} \quad \text{or} \quad F_1 = F_{(non;1;1)}$$

and

$$F_2 = F_{(id;1;1)} \quad \text{or} \quad F_2 = F_{(non;1;0)}.$$

Therefore one of the following cases appears:

$$M \supseteq [\widetilde{T}_0 \cup \{F_{(id;1;0)}, F_{(id;1;1)}\}] = K_1,$$

$$M \supseteq [\widetilde{T}_1 \cup \{F_{(id;1;0)}, F_{(id;1;1)}\}] = K_2,$$

$$M \supseteq [\widetilde{T}_0 \cup \{F_{(non;1;0)}, F_{(id;1;0)}\}] = K_3,$$

$$M \supseteq [\widetilde{T}_1 \cup \{F_{(non;1;0)}, F_{(id;1;0)}\}] = K_4,$$

$$M \supseteq [\widetilde{T}_0 \cup \{F_{(non;1;1)}, F_{(id;1;1)}\}] = K_5,$$

$$M \supseteq [\widetilde{T}_1 \cup \{F_{(non;1;1)}, F_{(id;1;1)}\}] = K_6,$$

$$M \supseteq [\widetilde{T}_0 \cup \{F_{(non;1;1)}, F_{(non;1;0)}\}] = K_7,$$

$$M \supseteq [\widetilde{T}_1 \cup \{F_{(non;1;1)}, F_{(non;1;0)}\}] = K_8.$$

We prove some relations:

vi) $[\widetilde{T}_0 \cup \{F_{(id;1;1)}\}] = K_1$ since the logical net of Figure 19 satisfies $F_N = F_{(id;1;0)}$.

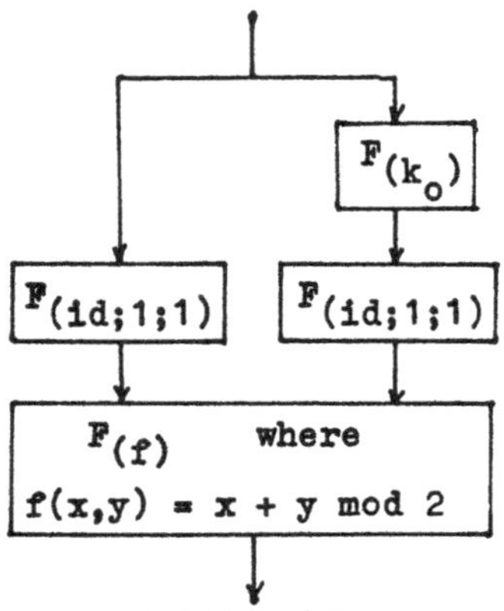

Figure 19

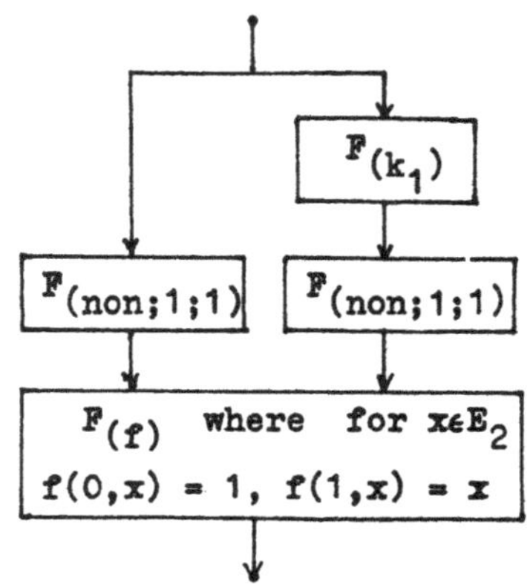

Figure 20

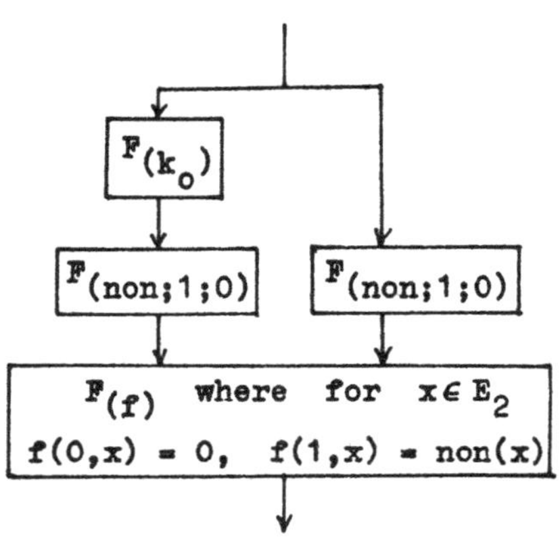

Figure 21

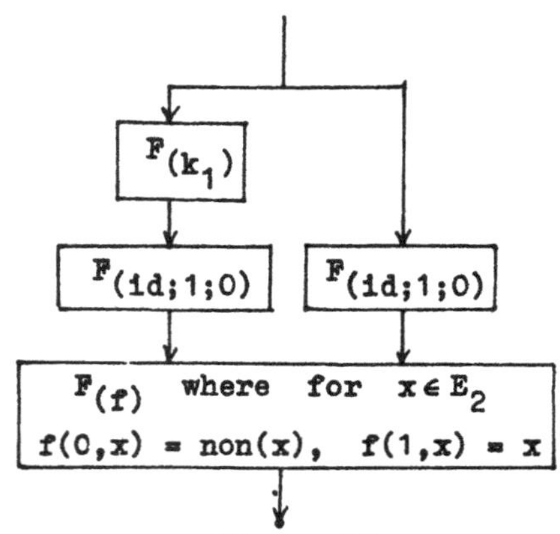

Figure 22

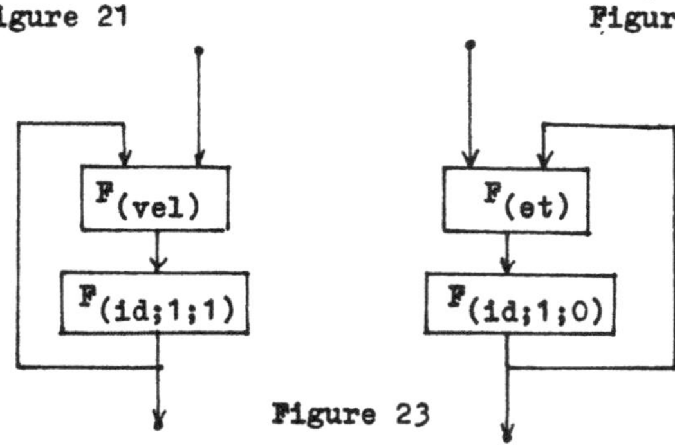

Figure 23

vii) $[\widetilde{T}_1 \cup \{F_{(non;1;1)}\}] = K_6$ because the function induced by the net of Figure 20 coincides with $F_{(id;1;1)}$.

viii) $[\widetilde{T}_o \cup \{F_{(non;1;0)}\}] = K_3$ since the net of Figure 21 satisfies $F_N = F_{(id;1;0)}$.

ix) $F_{(id;1;1)} \in [\widetilde{T}_1 \cup \{F_{(id;1;0)}\}]$ holds by Figure 22.

Therefore

$$K_5 \supseteq K_1, \quad K_8 \supseteq K_6, \quad K_7 \supseteq K_3, \text{ and } K_4 \supseteq K_2.$$

The induced functions of the nets of Figure 23 are equal to $F_{(k_1)}$ and $F_{(k_0)}$, respectively. Thus $F_{(k_1)} \in K_1$ and $F_{(k_0)} \in K_2$. Hence $K_1 = K_2 = P_2$. This implies $M \supseteq K_3$ or $M \supseteq K_6$, i.e. the lemma holds.

<u>Lemma 5.8.</u> i) $M_{T_0} = [\widetilde{T}_0 \cup \{F_{(non;1;0)}\}]$.

ii) $M_{T_1} = [\widetilde{T}_1 \cup \{F_{(non;1;1)}\}]$.

<u>Proof</u>. We prove the lemma for M_{T_0} only, because the steps in the proof of ii) are analogous. Let $F \in M_{T_0}$. Then there is an automaton $\mathfrak{A} = (E_2{}^n, E_2, Z, g, f, z_0)$ such that $F = F_{\mathfrak{A}}$. We code the set Z of states by tupels of $E_2{}^s$, where $2^{s-1} < |Z| \leq 2^s$. Without loss of generality we code z_0 by $(0,0,\ldots,0)$. Then we can describe $\mathfrak{A}$ as follows:

$$y = f(x_1,x_2,\ldots,x_n,q_1,q_2,\ldots,q_s),$$

$$(q_1{}',q_2{}',\ldots,q_s{}') = g(x_1,x_2,\ldots,x_n,q_1,q_2,\ldots,q_s),$$

$$q_i{}' = g_i(x_1,x_2,\ldots,x_n,q_1,q_2,\ldots,q_s) \quad \text{for } i = 1,2,\ldots,s,$$

where $f, g_1,g_2,\ldots,g_s$ are functions of $P_2^!$. Since $F \in M_{T_0}$, we have $f \in T_0$. Therefore $F_{(f)}$ is in $\widetilde{T}_0$. If $g_i \in T_0$, then $F_{(g_i)} \in \widetilde{T}_0$. If $g_i \notin T_0$, then $non \circ g_i \in T_0$ and thus $F_{(non \circ g_i)} \in \widetilde{T}_0$. By viii) of the proof of the last lemma $F_{(id;1;0)} \in [\widetilde{T}_0 \cup \{F_{(non;1;0)}\}]$. We now can modify the construction of Figure 3 in the following way. If $g_i \notin T_0$, we use $F_{(non;1;0)}$ as the delay element. Then we obtain that the constructed net induces F. We conclude that $M_{T_0} \supseteq [\widetilde{T}_0 \cup \{F_{(non;1;0)}\}]$. The converse inclusion is obvious.

<u>Theorem 5.9.</u> $M \subseteq P_2$ is a Kleene-set in P_2 if and only if $M = M_{T_0}$ or $M = M_{T_1}$ or $M = P_2$.

<u>Proof</u>. M_{T_0}, M_{T_1}, and P_2 are Kleene-sets by Examples 5.4. and 5.5.. Now let M be a Kleene-set in P_2. By Lemma 5.7. and Lemma 5.8., $M \supseteq M_{T_0}$ or $M \supseteq M_{T_1}$. $\underline{T_0}$ and $\underline{T_1}$ are maximal subalgebras of $\underline{P_2^!}$. Hence M_{T_0} and M_{T_1} are also maximal in $\underline{P_2}$ by Example 4.1.. Therefore $M = M_{T_0}$, $M = M_{T_1}$ or $M = P_2$.

The following lemma is a sligth generalization of Theorem 5.9.. For the definition of $N_{\{0,1\}}$ we refer to Example 5.6..

<u>Lemma 5.10.</u> A subalgebra $\underline{M} \subseteq \underline{N_{\{0,1\}}}$ is a Kleene-set in P_k if and only if $M = N_{\{0,1\}} \cap M_{T_0}$ or $M = N_{\{0,1\}} \cap M_{T_1}$ or $M = N_{\{0,1\}}$.

We omit the proof which can be given analogous to that of the above statements using results of /BDHL/ (a proof can be found in /Da6/).

With each $F \in P_2{}^n$, $n \in \mathbb{N}$, we associate a function $G_F \in P_k{}^n$, $k \geq 2$, as follows:

$$\varphi^{i}_{G_F}(a_1,a_2,\dots,a_i) = \begin{cases} \varphi^{i}_{F}(a_1,a_2,\dots,a_i) & \text{if } a_j \in \{0,1\}^n,\ 1 \leq j \leq i \\ 0 & \text{otherwise.} \end{cases}$$

Further, for a set $M \subseteq P_2$, we put

$$G_M = \{G_F : F \in M\} \cup \{F_{(h_i)} : i = 2,3,\dots,k-2\}$$

where h_i is defined by

$$h_i(0) = h_i(i) = 1, \quad h_i(j) = 0 \text{ for } j \notin \{0,i\}.$$

<u>Lemma 5.11.</u> $M \subseteq P_2$ is complete in $\underline{P_2}$ if and only if G_M is complete in $\underline{N_{\{0,1\}}}$.

<u>Proof</u>. For $H \in N_{\{0,1\}}$, let $\mathrm{pr}\, H$ be the restriction of H on $\{0,1\}^*$. It is easy to see that pr is a homomorphism from $N_{\{0,1\}}$ onto P_2. Hence $\mathrm{pr}[M'] = [\mathrm{pr}\, M']$ holds for each subset M' of $N_{\{0,1\}}$. Now let M be complete in $\underline{P_2}$. Then $F_{(et)}$, $F_{(non)}$, $F_{(aut)}$ (aut denotes the addition mod 2), and $F_{(id;1;0)}$ are contained in $[M]$. Hence we can construct these functions starting with functions of M. In the same way we can construct functions G_1, G_2, G_3, G_4 starting with functions of G_M such that

$$\mathrm{pr}(G_1) = F_{(et)},\ \mathrm{pr}(G_2) = F_{(non)},\ \mathrm{pr}(G_3) = F_{(aut)},$$
$$\mathrm{pr}(G_4) = F_{(id;1;0)}.$$

We define the functions j_i, $i = 1,2,\dots,k-2$, by

$$j_i(s) = \begin{cases} 1 & \text{if } s = i \\ 0 & \text{otherwise,} \end{cases}$$

and we obtain

$$F_{(j_1)}(p) = G_3(F_{(h_1)}(p), F_{(h_1)}(p)).$$

By the results of /BDHL/, we have

$$[G_M] \supseteq \{F_{(f)} : f \in P_{k,2}\}$$

where $P_{k,2}$ is the set of all functions of $P_K^!$ whose range is contained in E_2. By a sligth modification of the proof of Lemma 2.4. we can prove that

$$N_{\{0,1\}} = [\{G_1, G_2, G_3, G_4\} \cup \{F_{(j_i)} : i = 1,2,\ldots,k-2\}] \subseteq [G_M].$$

Hence G_M is complete in $\underline{N_{\{0,1\}}}$.

Now we suppose that G_M is complete in $\underline{N_{\{0,1\}}}$ and M is not complete in $\underline{P_2}$. Let F be a sequential function of P_2 which is not in $[M]$. But there is a function $G \in N_{\{0,1\}}$ with $\text{pr}\, G = F$. Therefore

$$F = \text{pr}\, G \in \text{pr}\,[G_M] = [\text{pr}\, G_M] = [M \cup \{F_{(id)}\}].$$

Obviously, M is complete in $\underline{P_2}$ if and only if $M \cup \{F_{(id)}\}$ is complete in $\underline{P_2}$ (see Lemma 2.9.). Thus we have obtained a contradiction.

Theorem 5.12. It is undecidable whether or not a finite set contained in P_k is Kleene-complete.

Proof. Suppose the Kleene-completeness in P_k is decidable for some $k \geq 2$. Let M be an arbitrary subset of P_2. We construct G_M. By Lemma 5.10., G_M is complete in $N_{\{0,1\}}$ if and only if G_M is Kleene-complete and if it is not contained in M_{T_0} and M_{T_1}. Obviously, it is decidable whether or not G_M contains $F_1 \notin M_{T_0}$ and $F_2 \notin M_{T_1}$. Thus, by our assumption, the completeness of G_M in $\underline{N_{\{0,1\}}}$ is decidable. By Lemma 5.11., the completeness of M in $\underline{P_2}$ is decidable. This contradicts Theorem 4.16..

The three completeness concepts regarded above have undecidable completeness problems in common. We now show that there are differences with respect to the algebraic approach using maximal noncomplete subalgebras and with respect to the generation of complete subalgebras (compare with Theorem 4.14., Theorem 5.3., and Theorem 4.2., Theorem 5.1.).

A subalgebra $\underline{M} \subseteq \underline{P_k}$ is called a pre-Kleene-set if and only if

i) M is not a Kleene-set in P_k,
ii) for each $F \notin M$, $[M \cup \{F\}]$ is a Kleene-set in P_k.

<u>Theorem 5.13.</u> i) A subset of P_k is Kleene-complete if and only if it is not contained in any pre-Kleene-set of P_k.
ii) The cardinality of the set of all pre-Kleene-sets of P_k is $\mathfrak{c}$.

We omit the proof since it uses some necessary preliminaries for $k \geq 3$ and refer to /Da7/, /Da10/.

<u>Theorem 5.14.</u> i) If $k = 2$, then every Kleene-set is finitely generated.
ii) If $k \geq 3$, there are Kleene-sets M_1, M_2, M_3 such that M_1 is finitely generated, M_2 has an infinite basis, and M_3 has no basis.

<u>Proof</u>. i) By Theorem 5.9., we have only three Kleene-sets in P_2 and they are finitely generated by Theorem 4.1.,and Lemma 5.8. and the results of /JGK/.
ii) We give the proof for $k = 3$.

We choose $M_1 = P_3$.
We consider the constant sequential functions C_t , $t \geq 1$, given by

$$\varphi^j_{C_t} = \begin{cases} k_1 & \text{if } k \neq t \\ k_2 & \text{if } k = t. \end{cases}$$

Then $M_2 = N_{\{0,1\}} \cup [\{C_t : t \geq 1\}]$ is a Kleene-set. $N_{\{0,1\}}$ is finitely generated by Lemma 5.11. Now we can show that M_2 has a basis as in the proof of Theorem 4.11..
We define the functions $F_i \in {P_k}^i$, $i \geq 1$, by

$$\varphi^1_{F_i} = k_2, \quad \varphi^t_{F_i} = k_0 \quad \text{for} \quad t \geq 3,$$

$$\varphi^2_{F_i}(x_1(1),\ldots,x_i(1),x_1(2),\ldots,x_i(2)) =$$

$$= \begin{cases} 0 & \text{if } x_j(1) \in \{0,1\} \text{ for } j = 1,2,\ldots,i \\ 2 & \text{if } x_j(1) = 2 \text{ for } j = 1,2,\ldots,i \\ 1 & \text{otherwise} \end{cases}$$

and put

$$M_3 = [N_{\{0,1\}} \cup \{F_i : i \geq 1\}].$$

We prove that M_3 has no basis. Using Δ it can be proved that F_j generates F_i if $i < j$. Therefore it suffices to prove that

$F_j \notin [\{F_{i_1},F_{i_2},\dots,F_{i_r}\} \cup N_{\{0,1\}}]$ if $j > \max\{i_1,i_2,\dots,i_r\}$. Suppose the contrary. Let (F_j) be the logical net which induces F_j and which is constructed in analogy to the operations in the generation of F_j from $\{F_{i_1},F_{i_2},\dots,F_{i_r}\} \cup N_{\{0,1\}}$. The last logical subnet in this construction has to induce a function F_i for some $i \in \{i_1,i_2,\dots,i_r\}$. If all input lines of this net (F_i) are connected with output lines of nets which induce elements of $N_{\{0,1\}}$, then $\varphi^2_{F_j} = k_0$, which contradicts its definition. If all input lines are connected with nets which induce a function of $\{F_{i_1},F_{i_2},\dots,F_{i_r}\}$, then $\varphi^2_{F_j} = k_2$, and we obtain a contradiction again. Therefore assume that at least one input line of (F_i) is connected with a net (F_{i_s}) for some s and at least one input line is connected with a net (F), $F \in N_{\{0,1\}}$. Then $\varphi^2_{F_j} = k_1$ which is impossible, too. Therefore at least one input line of (F_i) is also an input line of (F_j). Without loss of generality we assume that the nets have the first n input lines in common. The remaining input lines have to be connected either all with nets (F), $F \in N_{\{0,1\}}$, or all with nets of $\{(F_{i_1}),(F_{i_2}),\dots,(F_{i_r})\}$. In the first of these cases we have

$$\varphi^2_{F_j}(2,2,\dots,2,x_1(2),\dots,x_j(2)) = 1$$

for all $x_j(2) \in E_3$, and in the second case we obtain

$$\varphi^2_{F_j}(0,0,\dots,0,x_1(2),\dots,x_j(2)) = 1$$

independent of the inputs at the time moment 2. Again, this contradicts the definition of F_j.

<u>Theorem 5.15.</u> Any Kleene-complete set contains a finite Kleene-complete set.

<u>Proof</u>. For $k = 2$, the statement follows from the fact that M_{T_0}, M_{T_1}, and P_2 are finitely generated and Lemma 1.2.. For $k \geq 3$, we refer to /Da 8/, /Da11/.

Finally in this paragraph we shall discuss combinations of Kleene-completeness and metric completeness. We can introduce a metric
- on the set of sequential functions as in paragraph 5.1. or
- on the set of regular sets.

This can be done as follows: For two regular sets R, $S \subseteq (E_k{}^n)^+$, we define the distance

$$d'(R,S) = \min \{ l(p) : p \in (R \setminus S) \cup (S \setminus R) \} .$$

$M \subseteq P_k$ is called m_1-Kleene-complete if and only if, for any $\varepsilon > 0$ and any regular set R, there are functions F, $G \in P_k$ such that F accepts R, $G \in [M]$, and $d(F,G) < \varepsilon$.

$M \subseteq P_k$ is called m_2-Kleene-complete if and only if, for any $\varepsilon > 0$ and any regular set R, there are a function $F \in [M]$ and a regular set S such that S is accepted by F and $d'(R,S) < \varepsilon$.

The following lemma is easy to prove.

Lemma 5.16. A subset of P_k is m_1-Kleene-complete if and only if it is m_2-Kleene-complete.

Therefore, in the sequel we shall use the notion of m-Kleene-completeness.

Theorem 5.17. The m-Kleene-completeness of a finite subset of P_k is undecidable.

Proof. Again, we can show that M is m-complete in P_2 if and only if M is m-Kleene-complete and is not contained in M_{T_0} and M_{T_1} (for a detailed proof we refer to /Da4/). This gives the undecidability of m-Kleene-completeness in P_2. For $k \geq 3$, we have to modify Lemma 5.11. accordingly.

5.3. Delayed Completeness

We say that the sequential function G describes the sequential function F with delay σ, $\sigma \geq 0$, iff, for $i > \sigma$,

$$\varphi_G^i(x_1(1),\dots,x_n(1),\dots,x_1(i),\dots,x_n(i))$$
$$= \varphi_F^{i-\sigma}(x_1(1),\dots,x_n(1),\dots,x_1(i-\sigma),\dots,x_n(i-\sigma)).$$

Let $\sigma \geq 0$. $M \subseteq P_k$ is called σ-complete iff, for each function $F \in P_k$, there is a function $G \in [M]$ which describes F with delay σ.
M is called delayed complete (d-complete) iff there is an integer $\sigma \geq 0$ such that M is σ-complete.

Clearly, if $\sigma = 0$, we obtain the usual completeness. In this paragraph we prove

Theorem 5.18. It is undecidable whether or not a finite set contained in P_k is d-complete.

Proof. We give the proof for $k = 2$.
First we introduce some notations. Let p be an arbitrary word over $\{0,1\}$ with $l(p) = r > 0$. We define the function $U_p \in P_2{}^3$ by

$$U_p((x_1(1),x_2(1),x_3(1)),\ldots,(x_1(i),x_2(i),x_3(i)))$$

$$= \begin{cases} 0^{j+r} sh(x_1(j+r+1),x_2(j+r+1))\ldots sh(x_1(i),x_2(i)) \\ \qquad \text{if } x_3(1)x_3(2)\ldots x_3(j+r) = 0^j p \text{ for some } j \\ 0^i \qquad \text{otherwise .} \end{cases}$$

Claim. Let $M \subseteq P_2$ contain the functions $F_{(id;1;0)}$ and U_p for some p. If $[M]$ contains a certain constant sequential function C_β with $\beta(1)\beta(2)\ldots\beta(j+r) = 0^j p$, then M is d-complete.

Proof of the claim. $F_{(sh)}$, $F_{(id;1;0)}$ is complete in $\underline{P_2}$. Therefore any $F \in P_2$ can be generated from $F_{(sh)}$ and $F_{(id;1;0)}$. We now replace in this construction each $F_{(sh)}$ by U_p. For all variables corresponding to the third variables of the U_p's we substitute the constant C_β. Evidently, the function constructed in this way describes F with delay $j+r$.

Now let $T = (u_1 \to v_1,\ u_2 \to v_2, \ldots,\ u_n \to v_n)$ be a semi-Thue-system. We code the words u_i, v_i, $1 \le i \le n$, by words over $\{0,1\}$ and obtain the rules in the form

$$u(1)u(2)\ldots u(s) \to v(1)v(2)\ldots v(t)$$

where without loss of generality $u(1) = u(s) = v(1) = v(t) = 1$. With such a rule we associate the sequential function $F \in P_2{}^1$ which is defined by

$$F(x(1)x(2)\ldots x(i))$$

$$= \begin{cases} 0^s x(1)x(2)\ldots x(l)v(1)v(2)\ldots v(t)x(l+s)x(l+s+1)\ldots x(i-t) \\ \qquad \text{if } x(l+1)x(l+2)\ldots x(l+s) \text{ is the first appearance} \\ \qquad \text{of } u(1)u(2)\ldots u(s) \text{ in } x(1)x(2)\ldots x(i) \\ 0^s x(1)x(2)\ldots x(i-s) \qquad \text{otherwise.} \end{cases}$$

We now consider the set $M = \{F_{(id;1;0)}, U_p, F_1, F_2, \ldots, F_n\}$, where the functions F_i, $1 \le i \le n$, are associated with the coded rules $u_i \to v_i$. It is easy to see that the only constant function in $[M]$ is $F_{(k_0)}$.

Let $p \notin \{0\}^*$. Then $[M]$ contains no constant function C_β where $\beta = 0^j p\ldots$ for some j. For $q \in \{0,1\}^*$, $q = x_1 x_2 \ldots x_u$, let H_q be the sequential function defined by

$$\varphi^i_{H_q} = \begin{cases} k_{x_i} & \text{if } i \leq u \\ k_o & \text{if } i > u. \end{cases}$$

Then $[M \cup \{H_q\}]$ contains a function C_α with $\alpha = 0^k p\ldots$ for some k if and only if p can be derived from q in T. By the claim, $[M \cup \{H_q\}]$ is d-complete if and only if p can be generated from q in T. Therefore the d-completeness is undecidable, by the results of paragraph 1.2..

5.4. Strongly Connected Input Divided Automata

Up to now, all modifications have led to a weaker concept of completeness where the modified completeness problem is undecidable. The only exception was t-completeness, $t > 0$, but a t-complete set does not generate a subalgebra which can be considered as a representative for the algebra $\underline{P_k}$. In this paragraph we shall make a restriction on the set M which is under consideration such that it will be decidable whether or not $[M] = P_k$. For simplicity, we shall suppose $k = 2$ again.

Our restriction is as follows: M contains only strongly connected input divided automata. First we define this type of automaton.

$\mathfrak{A} = (E_2{}^n, E_2, Z, g, f, z_o)$ is strongly connected input divided if and only if the following conditions are satisfied:

i) for each state $z, z' \in Z$, there is a input $(x_1, x_2, \ldots, x_n) \in E_2{}^n$ such that

$$g(z,(x_1,x_2,\ldots,x_n)) = z',$$

ii) there is a number r, $1 \leq r \leq n$ such that

$$f(z,(x_1,x_2,\ldots,x_n)) = f'(z,x_1,x_2,\ldots,x_r),$$
$$g(z,(x_1,x_2,\ldots,x_n)) = g'(z,x_{r+1},x_{r+2},\ldots,x_n),$$

i.e. f essentially depends only on $x_1, x_2, \ldots, x_r$ and g essentially depends only on $x_{r+1}, x_{r+2}, \ldots, x_n$.

Condition i) describes the strong connectedness of the automaton, by ii) the input lines are divided into two types. The first r variables are called variables of the first type, the last $n-r$ variables are

variables of second type.
The purpose of this paragraph is to prove the following theorem (for the definitions of the used subalgebras see the examples in paragraph 2.3.).

> Theorem 5.19. Let M be a set of sequential functions which are induced by strongly connected input divided automata.
> i) Then M is complete in $\underline{P_2}$ if and only if M is not contained in the sets M_{T_0}, M_{T_1}, M_L, $M_{\mathcal{M}}$, M_S, and M^2.
> ii) It is decidable whether or not M is complete.

Proof. ii) follows from i) because it is decidable whether or not a function is contained in M_R, $R \subseteq P_2^!$, and M^2 by the definitions of these sets.
The necessity of the condition in i) is obvious since $\underline{M_{T_1}}$, $\underline{M_{T_0}}$, $\underline{M_L}$, $\underline{M_{\mathcal{M}}}$, $\underline{M_S}$, and $\underline{M^2}$ are (maximal) subalgebras of $\underline{P_2}$. Therefore we have only to prove that the condition is sufficient.
Let M be not contained in M_{T_0}, M_{T_1}, M_L, $M_{\mathcal{M}}$, M_S, and M^2. We prove the following two claims.

Claim 1. Let $f \in P_2^!$. Then $F_{(f)} \in [M]$.

Claim 2. $F_{(id;1;0)} \in [M]$.

By these two claims and the fact that $\{F_{(sh)}, F_{(id;1;0)}\}$ is complete the statement is proved.

Proof of claim 1. We have sequential functions $F_i \in M$, $1 \le i \le 6$, induced by strongly connected input divided automata such that

$$F_1 \notin M_{T_0},\quad F_2 \notin M_{T_1},\quad F_3 \notin M_L,\quad F_4 \notin M_{\mathcal{M}},\quad F_5 \notin M_S,\quad F_6 \in M^2.$$

By definition, we have

$$\varphi^1_{F_1} \notin T_0,\quad \varphi^1_{F_2} \notin T_1,\quad \varphi^1_{F_3} \notin L,\quad \varphi^1_{F_4} \notin \mathcal{M},\quad \varphi^1_{F_5} \notin S.$$

By Lemma 3.5., we obtain that, for each function $f \in P_2^!$, we can construct a function $H(f) \in [M]$ such that $\varphi^1_{H(f)}$ and f differ only in dummy variables. Especially $H(f)$ has all variables of second type of all functions used in the construction as variables of second type,
We consider $H_1 = H(k_0)$ and $H_2 = H(k_1)$. Let the first variable of H_1 and H_2 be of first type, and let $x_2, x_3, \ldots, x_m$ and $x_2, x_3, \ldots x_n$ be the variables of second type of H_1 and H_2, respectively. By the strong connectedness of H_1 and H_2 there are

tuples $(a_2,a_3,\dots,a_m)$ and $(b_2,b_3,\dots,b_n)$ such that

$$g_{H_1}(z_{o1},(a_2,a_3,\dots,a_m)) = z_{o1},\quad g_{H_2}(z_{o2},(b_2,b_3,\dots,b_n)) = z_{o2}$$

hold for the automata associated with H_1 and H_2, respectively (where z_{o1} and z_{o2} denote the initial states). We identify all variables with $a_i = 1$ and all variables with $a_k = 0$ and obtain a function H_1' such that

$$\varphi^1_{H_1'} = k_o \quad \text{and} \quad g_{H_1'}(z'_{o1},(1,0)) = z'_{o1} .$$

Analogously we construct H_2' with

$$\varphi^1_{H_2'} = k_1 \quad \text{and} \quad g_{H_2'}(z'_{o2},(1,0)) = z'_{o2} .$$

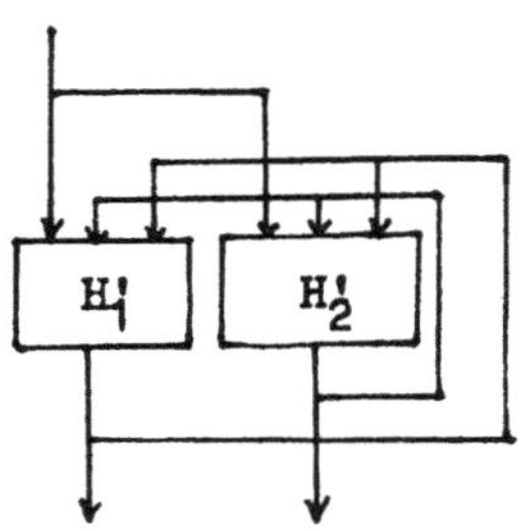

Figure 24

Then the net N given in Figure 24 induces the constant mappings $F_{(k_o)}$ and $F_{(k_1)}$ on the first and second output line, respectively.

Let f be an arbitrary function of $P_2'^s$. By the above argument we can construct $H(f)$. Then the first s variables of $H(f)$ are of first type. Let the last t variables be of second type (i.e. $H(f) \in P_2^{t+s}$). Again, there are elements $c_1,c_2,\dots,c_t$ such that

$$g_{H(f)}(z_o,(c_1,c_2,\dots,c_t)) = z_o .$$

Again, we identify the variables according to the values of the c_i's. Then the net of Figure 25 induces $F_{(f)}$.

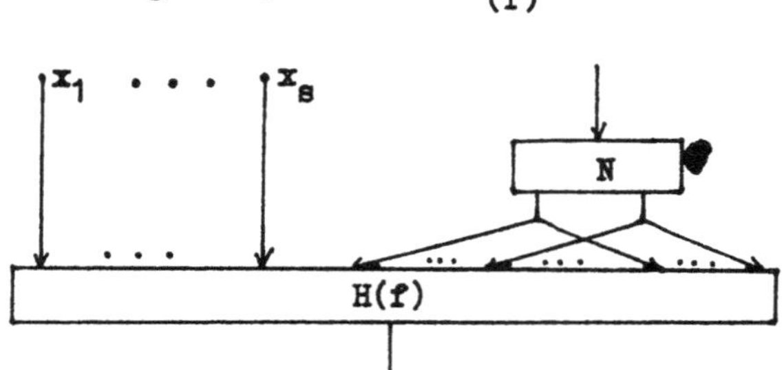

Figure 25

Proof of Claim 2. Let F_6 be the function of M with $F_6 \in M^2$. Let the first r variables be of first type and the last s variables of second type. Since $F_6 \in M^2$ and F_6 is strongly connected input divided, there are tuples $(d_{r+1}, d_{r+2}, \ldots, d_{r+s})$, $(d'_{r+1}, d'_{r+2}, \ldots, d'_{r+s})$, $(d''_1, d''_2, \ldots, d''_r)$ such that

$$g(z_o, (d_{r+1}, d_{r+2}, \ldots, d_{r+s})) = z_1,\ g(z_o, (d'_{r+1}, d'_{r+2}, \ldots, d'_{r+s})) = z_2,$$

$$f(z_1, (d''_1, d''_2, \ldots, d''_r)) \neq f(z_2, (d''_1, d''_2, \ldots, d''_r)).$$

Let $f(z_1, (d''_1, d''_2, \ldots, d''_r)) = a = 0$. Further let $(d^{i,j}_{r+1}, d^{i,j}_{r+2}, \ldots, d^{i,j}_{r+s})$ be the tuple such that

$$g(z_i, (d^{i,j}_{r+1}, d^{i,j}_{r+2}, \ldots, d^{i,j}_{r+s})) = z_j.$$

By Claim 1, $F_{(k_{d''_i})} \in [M]$ for $1 \leq i \leq r$, and thus we can construct the net N' of Figure 26. Obviously,

$$\varphi^1_{F_{N'}}(x_1, x_{r+1}, x_{r+2}, \ldots, x_{r+s}) = f_{N'}(d''_1, d''_2, \ldots, d''_r) = b,$$

and hence $\varphi^1_{F_{N'}}$ is a constant mapping. Let $b = 0$.

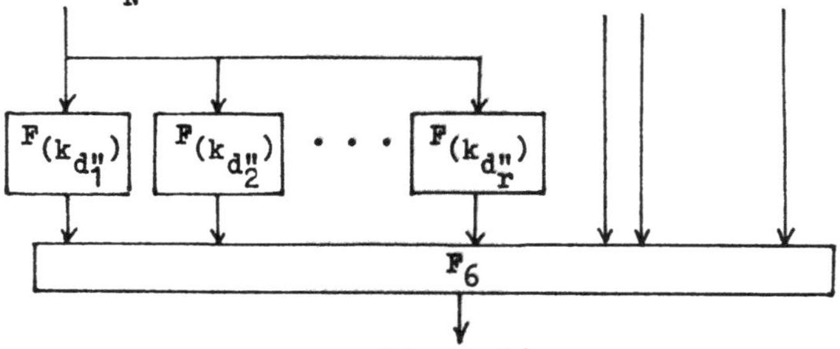

Figure 26

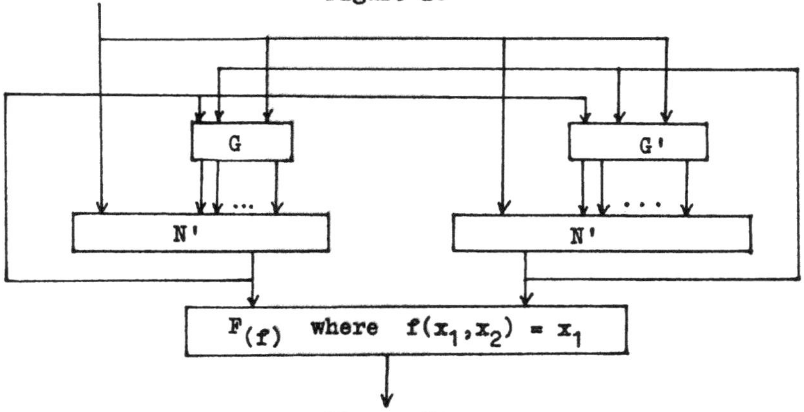

Figure 27

By Claim 1, we can construct the sequential functions $F_{(g_i)}$, $F_{(g_i')}$ of $P_2^{\,3}$ where

$$g_i(x_1,x_2,x_3) = \begin{cases} d_{r+i} & \text{if } x_1 = x_2 = x_3 = 0 \\ d'_{r+i} & \text{if } x_1 = x_2 = 0,\ x_3 = 1 \\ d^{1,1}_{r+i} & \text{if } x_1 = x_3 = 0,\ x_2 = 1 \\ d^{1,2}_{r+i} & \text{if } x_1 = 0,\ x_2 = x_3 = 1 \\ d^{2,1}_{r+i} & \text{if } x_1 = x_2 = x_3 = 1 \\ d^{2,2}_{r+i} & \text{if } x_1 = x_3 = 1,\ x_2 = 0 \\ \text{arbitrary} & \text{otherwise} \end{cases}$$

$$g_i'(x_1,x_2,x_3) = \begin{cases} d'_{r+i} & \text{if } x_1 = x_2 = x_3 = 0 \\ d_{r+i} & \text{if } x_1 = x_2 = 0,\ x_3 = 1 \\ d^{1,2}_{r+i} & \text{if } x_1 = x_3 = 0,\ x_2 = 1 \\ d^{1,1}_{r+i} & \text{if } x_1 = 0,\ x_2 = x_3 = 1 \\ d^{2,2}_{r+i} & \text{if } x_1 = 0,\ x_2 = x_3 = 0 \\ d^{2,1}_{r+i} & \text{if } x_1 = x_3 = 1,\ x_2 = 0 \\ \text{arbitrary} & \text{otherwise} \end{cases}$$

for $1 \leq i \leq s$. Let G and G' be the vector functions $G = (F_{(g_1)}, F_{(g_2)}, \ldots, F_{(g_s)})$ and $G' = (F_{(g_1')}, F_{(g_2')}, \ldots, F_{(g_s')})$. Then the induced function of the net of Figure 27 is in $[M]$, and it coincides with $F_{(id;1;0)}$.
If $(a,b) \neq (0,0)$, we have to modify the latter construction slightly.

5.5. I-Completeness

In this paragraph we shall give a decidable modification of s-completeness. We restrict ourselves to $k = 2$.
We say that an automaton $\mathfrak{A} = (E_2^{\,n}, E_2, Z, g, f, z_0)$ is an I-automaton, iff, for every $z \in Z$, there is an integer i, $1 \leq i \leq n$, such that

$$f(z,(x_1,x_2,\ldots,x_n)) = f_z(x_1,x_2,\ldots,x_n) = h(x_i)$$

where $h \in P_2^{!1}$ depends on z. We put

$$D = \{F_{\mathfrak{A}} : \mathfrak{A} \text{ is an I-automaton}\}.$$

A set $M \subseteq P_2$ is I-complete in P_2 if and only if $[D \cup M]_s = P_2$.

Lemma 5.19. There are finite I-complete sets in P_2.

Proof. By the proof of Lemma 4.8., we have $[D \cup \{F_{(sh)}\}]_s = P_2$.

We introduce some characters of an automaton associated with a sequential function and use them to obtain a criterion of I-completeness which implies an algorithm.

Let $\mathfrak{A} = (E_2^n, E_2, Z, g, f, z_o)$, $z \in Z$, $a \in E_2^n$, $A \subseteq E_2^n$. By f_z we denote the function defined by .

$$f_z(x_1, x_2, \ldots, x_n) = f(z, (x_1, x_2, \ldots, x_n)).$$

z is called a-cyclic iff there is a word $p \in (E_2^n)^*$ such that $g(z, ap) = z$, and z is A-cyclic iff it is a-cyclic for all $a \in A$. The pair (f_z, A) is called a z-pair in $\mathfrak{A}$ iff z is A-cyclic. Further we put

$$Z^{(t)} = \{z : z \in Z,\ g(z_o, p) = z \text{ for some } p \in (E_2^n)^* \text{ with } l(p) = t\}.$$

An (n,m)-operator V is an n-tuple $V = (v_1, v_2, \ldots, v_n)$ where $v_1, v_2, \ldots, v_n$ are m-ary functions of $P_2^!$. We say that $a = (a_1, a_2, \ldots, a_n) \in E_2^n$ is realized by V iff there is a tuple $(b_1, b_2, \ldots, b_m) \in E_2^m$ such that $v_i(b_1, b_2, \ldots, b_m) = a_i$ for $1 \le i \le n$. $N(V)$ denotes the set of all elements of E_2^n which can be realized by V. If $f \in P_2^{!n}$, we define $f(V) \in P_2^{!m}$ by

$$f(V)(x_1, x_2, \ldots, x_m) = f(v_1(x_1, \ldots, x_m), \ldots, v_n(x_1, \ldots, x_m))$$

V is called unary iff any v_i, $1 \le i \le n$, essentially depends at most on one variable, and it is linear, iff any v_i, $1 \le i \le n$, is a linear function. Let $\mathcal{U}_n$ and $\mathcal{L}_n$ denote the set of all unary and linear $(n, 2^n)$-operators, respectively. The following statement can be proved easily.

Statement. i) For every unary (n,m)-operator V, there is a $V' \in \mathcal{U}_n$ such that $N(V) = N(V')$.
ii) For every linear (n,m)-operator V, there is a $V' \in \mathcal{L}_n$ such that $N(V) = N(V')$.

We define

$$P_t(\mathfrak{A}) = \{(z,V) : z \in Z^{(t)},\ V \in \mathcal{U}_n,\ N(V) \subseteq A \text{ and } (f_z,A) \text{ is a z-pair for some } A \neq \emptyset\},$$

$$\widetilde{P_t}(\mathfrak{A}) = \{(z,V) : (z,V) \in P_t(\mathfrak{A}),\ f_z(V) \text{ essentially depends at least on two variables}\},$$

$$D_t(\mathfrak{A}) = \{(z,V) : z \in Z^{(t)},\ V \in \mathcal{L}_n,\ N(V) \subseteq A \text{ and } (f_z,A) \text{ is a z-pair for some } A \neq \emptyset\},$$

$$\widetilde{D_t}(\mathfrak{A}) = \{(z,V) : (z,V) \in D_t(\mathfrak{A}),\ f_z(V) \text{ is nonlinear}\}.$$

Let $M = \{H_1,H_2,\ldots,H_n\} \subseteq P_2$. Let $\mathfrak{A}_i$ be an automaton with $F_{\mathfrak{A}_i} = H_i$, $1 \le i \le n$. We put $M' = \{\mathfrak{A}_1, \mathfrak{A}_2, \ldots, \mathfrak{A}_n\}$.

<u>Lemma 5.20.</u> Let M be I-complete. Then

i) for each $t \ge 0$, there is an automaton $\mathfrak{B} \in M'$ and a state z of $\mathfrak{B}$ such that f_z depends at least on two variables, $z \in Z^{(t)}$,

ii) there is a number t_0 such that $\bigcup_{\mathfrak{A} \in M'} \widetilde{P_t}(\mathfrak{A}) \neq \emptyset$ for $t \ge t_0$.

<u>Proof</u>. i) is obvious since, in the opposite case, we can generate from $M \cup D$ only functions whose associated automata satisfy the following condition: For every state z, f_z essentially depends at most on one variable.

Assume that ii) does not hold. Then there is an infinite sequence $t_1, t_2, \ldots$ of integers such that $0 < t_1 < t_2 < \ldots$ and $\bigcup_{\mathfrak{A} \in M'} \widetilde{P_{t_j}}(\mathfrak{A}) \neq \emptyset$ for $j = 1,2,\ldots$.

Since M is I-complete, we can composite from M' and the automata whose induced function is in D an automaton $\mathfrak{A}$ inducing $F_{(sh)}$. Let M_1 be the set of automata which are used in this construction.

We consider an arbitrary word $p = a_1a_2\ldots a_{t_1} \in (E_2{}^2)^*$ of length t_1. Then we regard the behaviour of $\mathfrak{A}$ at the (t_1+1)-th time moment. Each element of M_1 is in a state z such that

a) there is no letter a such that z is a-cyclic, or

b) $f_z(V)$ essentially depends at most on one variable for all unary (n,m)-operators V.

Now, let M_2 be the set of all automata of M_1 whose inputs are connected with inputs of $\mathfrak{A}$ or with outputs of a subcomposition which consists only of automata inducing a function of D. If M_2 is empty, then $\varphi_F^{t_1+1}(a_1,a_2,\ldots,a_{t_1},a_{t_1+1})$ essentially depends at most on one component of a_{t_1+1}. This implies $F_{\mathfrak{A}} \neq F_{(sh)}$. Therefore $M_2 \neq \emptyset$. If

a) holds for an element of M_2, then there is a letter $b \in E_2{}^2$ such that $R(p_1 b) < R(p_1)$, where

$$R(p) = |\{z : z = g(z_o, pq) \text{ for some } q \neq \lambda\}|.$$

If b) holds for all automata of M_2, we consider the set M_3 of all automata of M_1 whose inputs are inputs of $\mathfrak{A}$ or connected with outputs of a subcomposition which consists only of elements of M_2 and automata inducing a function of D. As above, we can show that $M_3 \neq \emptyset$. Again, if a) holds for an element of M_3, then $R(p_1 b) < R(p_1)$ for some b. In the opposite case, we proceed the construction of the sets $M_4, M_5, \ldots$. Since M_1 is finite the process halts in a finite number of steps. Therefore there has to be an element b with $R(p_1 b) < R(p_1)$, since $M_i \neq \emptyset$ for $i \geq 1$.
Then we consider p_2 such that $l(p_1 b p_2) = t_2$ and can prove by the same arguments that

$$R(p_1 b p_2 c) < R(p_1 b p_2) \leq R(p_1 b) < R(p_1) .$$

This process also halts in a finite number of steps because $\mathfrak{A}$ has a finite set of states. Therefore the above assumption is not valid.

<u>Lemma 5.21.</u> If M is I-complete, then
i) for each $t \geq 0$, there exist an automaton $\mathfrak{A} \in M'$ and a state z of $\mathfrak{A}$ such that f_z is nonlinear and $z \in Z^{(t)}$,
ii) there is an integer t_o such that $\bigcup_{\mathfrak{A} \in M'} \widetilde{D_t}(\mathfrak{A}) \neq \emptyset$ for $t \geq t_o$.

The proof of Lemma 5.21. can be given by the same arguments as in the proof of Lemma 5.20..

<u>Lemma 5.22.</u> If the set $M \subseteq P_2$ satisfies the conditions i) and ii) of Lemma 5.20., then $F_{(h)} \in [M \cup D]_s$ for all linear functions $h \in P_2'$.

<u>Proof</u>. By ii) there is an integer t_o and an automaton $\mathfrak{A} \in M'$ such that $P_{t_o}(\mathfrak{A}) \neq \emptyset$. Therefore $\mathfrak{A}$ has a state $z \in Z^{(t)}$, i.e. $z = g(z_o, p)$ for some $p = (p_1, p_2, \ldots, p_n)$, $p_i = b_{i1} b_{i2} \ldots b_{it_o}$, $1 \leq i \leq n$, and a unary (n,m)-operator $V = (v_1, v_2, \ldots, v_n)$ such that z is A-cyclic, $N(V) \subseteq A$, and $f_z(V)$ essentially depends at least on two variables. Hence there is a word p_a for $a = (a_1, a_2, \ldots, a_m) \in E_2{}^m$ such that $g(z, vp_a) = z$, where $v = (v_1(a_1, a_2, \ldots, a_m), v_2(a_1, a_2, \ldots, a_m), \ldots, v_n(a_1, a_2, \ldots, a_m))$. Let $l(vp_a) = r_a$ and $r = \prod_{a \in A} r_a$. Then $q_a = p_a v p_a v \ldots p_a v p_a$ is a word of length r-1 with $g(z, vq_a) = z$. Let $q_{a_i} = a_{i1} a_{i2} \ldots a_{i,r-1}$ for $i = 1, 2, \ldots, n$.

For $1 \leq i \leq n$, the functions F_i defined by

$$\varphi^j_{F_i}(c_1,c_2,\ldots,c_j) = \begin{cases} k_{b_{ij}} & \text{for } j \leq t_o \\ v_i(c_j) & \text{for } j = t_o+ur+1,\ u \geq 0 \\ k_{a_{is}} & \text{for } j = t_o+ur+s+1,\ u \geq 0 \end{cases}$$

are in D. We define G by

$$G(p) = F_{\mathfrak{A}}(F_1(p),F_2(p),\ldots,F_n(p)).$$

Then

$$\varphi^j_G(d_1,d_2,\ldots,d_j) = f(d_j) \quad \text{for} \quad j = t_o+ur+1,\ u \geq 0$$

for some $f \in P_2^!$, which depends at least on two variables. It is known that any linear function $h \in P_2^!$ can be generated from $\{f, k_o, \text{non}\}$. Therefore there is an $H \in [M \cup D]_s$ with

$$\varphi^j_H(d_1,d_2,\ldots,d_j) = h(d_j) \quad \text{for} \quad j = t_o+ur+1,\ u \geq 0.$$

An analogous construction can be given for $j = t_o + ur + s$, $1 \leq s \leq r$, and using i) of Lemma 5.20. we can also give it for integers smaller than t_o. Hence $F_{(h)} \in [M \cup D]_s$ for any linear function $h \in P_2^!$.

<u>Theorem 5.23.</u> $M \subseteq P_2$ is I-complete if and only if the following conditions are satisfied:

i) for each $t \geq 0$, there exist an automaton $\mathfrak{A} \in M'$ and a state z of $\mathfrak{A}$ such that $z \in Z^{(t)}$ and f_z is nonlinear,

ii) there is an integer t_o such that $\bigcup_{\mathfrak{A} \in M'} \widetilde{P}_t(\mathfrak{A}) \neq \emptyset$ and $\bigcup_{\mathfrak{A} \in M'} \widetilde{D}_t(\mathfrak{A}) \neq \emptyset$ for $t \geq t_o$.

Proof. The conditions are necessary by Lemma 5.20. and Lemma 5.21.. If i) and ii) are satisfied, we can generate $F_{(h)}$ for any linear function h by Lemma 5.22. since i) implies that f_z essentially depends at least on two variables. As in the proof of Lemma 5.22 we can generate a function $F_{(g)}$ where g is nonlinear. Hence $F_{(sh)} \in [M \cup D]_s$. Thus M is I-complete.

Note that Theorem 5.23. gives an analogon to the criterion of Słupecki in the case of functions over a finite set (Lemma 3.3.i)).

<u>Theorem 5.24.</u> The I-completeness of a finite set $M \subseteq P_2$ is decidable.

Proof. The sequences

$$Z^{(1)}, Z^{(2)}, \ldots, Z^{(t)}, \ldots ,$$

$$\widetilde{P_1}(\mathfrak{A}), \widetilde{P_2}(\mathfrak{A}), \ldots, \widetilde{P_t}(\mathfrak{A}), \ldots ,$$

$$\widetilde{D_1}(\mathfrak{A}), \widetilde{D_2}(\mathfrak{A}), \ldots, \widetilde{D_t}(\mathfrak{A}), \ldots$$

are periodic. Thus i) and ii) of Theorem 5.23. are decidable.

Exercises

1. Let $\varkappa$ be a one-to-one mapping of the words of length t over E_2 onto E_{2^t}. With $F \in P_2{}^n$ we associate the function $f(F) \in P'_{2^t}{}^n$ by

   $$f(a_1, \ldots, a_n) = b \quad \text{iff} \quad F(\varkappa^{-1}(a_1), \ldots, \varkappa^{-1}(a_n)) = \varkappa^{-1}(b).$$

   i) Prove that $M = \{f(F) : F \in P_k\}$ forms a subalgebra of $\underline{P'_2}$.
   ii) For $t = 1,2$, solve the completeness problem with respect to $\underline{M}$ by determination of all maximal subalgebras of $\underline{M}$ (cf. /Bu5/).

2. With $M \subseteq P_k$ we associate $N(t,M) \subseteq P_k$ by

   $N(t,M) = \{F : F \in P_k$, there is an $F' \in M$ such that $\varphi^i_F = \varphi^i_{F'}$, for $i \leq t\}$.

   Prove that $M = N(t,M)$ holds for any t-precomplete set.

3. Show that the set of Kleene-sets in P_k, $k \geq 3$, has the cardinality $\mathfrak{c}$ (cf. /Da6/).

4. $M \subseteq P_k$ is called a minimal Kleene-set iff it is a Kleene set and there is no Kleene-set which is properly contained in M. Prove that the set of minimal Kleene-sets in P_k, $k \geq 3$, has the cardinality $\aleph$ (cf /Da8/).

5. Prove that any Kleene-complete set contains a finite Kleene-complete set (cf /Da8/).

6. Show the existence of a d-complete set which is neither metrically complete nor Kleene-complete

7. Prove that it is decidable whether or not an automaton is strongly connected.

8. For $f,g \in P'^n_k$, $F,G \in P_k{}^n$, we define

   $$d'(f,g) = \frac{1}{2^n} \left| \{x : x \in E_k{}^n, f(x) \neq g(x)\} \right| , \quad d'(F,G) = \sum_{i=1}^{\infty} \frac{1}{2^i} d'(\varphi^i_F, \varphi^i_G).$$

   Prove that the associated metric completeness of a finite subset of P_k is undecidable (cf. /Da11/).

6. The Semigroup $P_k^{\ 1}$

Lemma 6.1. $(P_k^{\ 1}, \circ)$ is a semigroup.

In this chapter we shall study this semigroup. By the following facts it is of interest in connection with completeness problems.
By definition, $\zeta(F) = \tau(F) = \Delta(F) = F$ if $F \in P_k^{\ 1}$.
Concerning the operation $\times$ we note that $\times F$ is a constant mapping and it can be generated from two nonconstant mappings by using the substitution. If $\times F = C_\alpha$, we define F_1 and F_2 by

$$\varphi^1_{F_1}(x(1)) = x(1), \quad \varphi^i_{F_1} = k_{\alpha(i)} \quad \text{for } i \geq 2,$$

$$\varphi^1_{F_2} = k_{\alpha(1)}, \quad \varphi^i_{F_2}(x(1),x(2),\ldots,x(i)) = x(i) \quad \text{for } i \geq 2$$

and obtain $F_1 \circ F_2 = C_\alpha = \times F$. Since $F \circ C_\beta = C_\gamma$ and $C_\beta \circ F = C_\beta$ for any $F \in P_k^{\ 1}$, $C_\beta \in P_k^{\ 1}$, we can generate a nonconstant function only from nonconstant functions. Therefore we have the following

Statement. Let M be a subset of $P_k^{\ 1}$. If $[M] \supseteq P_k^{\ 1}$, then $[M \setminus (M \cap C)]_s \supseteq P_k^{\ 1}$, where C denotes the set of all constant unary sequential mappings.

The operation ∇ is used to generate all functions which differ in the number of dummy variables. If we identify all such functions, i.e. we regard completeness up to equivalence, it is not necessary to consider the operation ∇.
Hence we restrict ourselves to the operation $\circ$.

Theorem 6.2. The semigroup $(P_k^{\ 1}, \circ)$ is not finitely generated.

Proof. We can prove the theorem by the same method as in the proof of Theorem 4.5..

In contrast to Theorem 4.10., for $P_k^{\ 1}$, we have

Theorem 6.3. $(P_k^{\ 1}, \circ)$ is of type 2, i.e. any system of generators is reducible.

Proof. For a function $F \in P_k^{\ 1}$, let $I(F)$ denote the set of all $p \in E_k^{\ *}$ for which there exist letters x_1, x_2 with $x_1 \neq x_2$ and $F_p(x_1) = F_p(x_2)$. Further, let $J(F)$ be the set of all words $p \in I(F)$ such that each proper initial part of p is not in $I(F)$. If $\lambda \in I(F)$, let $J(F) = \{\lambda\}$.

We first prove the following

<u>Claim 1</u>. For any $F_1, F_2 \in P_k^1$, $p \in E_k^*$, if $p \notin J(F_1)$ and $F_1(p) \notin J(F_2)$, then $p \notin J(F_2 \circ F_1)$.

Proof of the claim. By the definition of $I(F)$, $p \in I(F_2 \circ F_1)$ if and only if $p \in I(F_1)$ or $F_1(p) \in I(F_2)$. Therefore $p \notin I(F_1)$ and $F_1(p) \notin I(F_2)$ imply $p \notin I(F_2 \circ F_1)$. Hence $p \notin J(F_2 \circ F_1)$.
Now suppose $p \in I(F_1) \setminus J(F_1)$. Then p has a proper initial part q with $q \in I(F_1)$. Therefore $q \in I(F_2 \circ F_1)$. Since q is a proper initial part of p, we obtain $p \notin J(F_2 \circ F_1)$.
Now let $F_1(p) \in I(F_2) \setminus J(F_2)$. Let r be a proper initial part of $F_1(p)$ such that $r \in I(F_2)$. Thus there is a proper initial part q of p with $F_1(q) = r$. Since $F_1(q) \in I(F_2)$, we have $q \in I(F_2 \circ F_1)$ and therefore $p \notin J(F_2 \circ F_1)$.

Let M be a system of generators of P_k^1. We show that there exists a function F in M with at least two elements in $J(F)$. Let N denote the set of all elements $G \in P_k^1$ for which $J(G)$ contains exactly one word. Let $F_1, F_2, \ldots, F_n \in N$. By Claim 1, we can prove that $J(F_1 \circ F_2 \circ \ldots \circ F_n)$ contains at most n elements. Thus we can only generate functions H' from N, where $J(H')$ is a finite set. Now, let x be a fixed element of E_k. It is easy to see that the function H defined by

$$\varphi_H^i(x(1), x(2), \ldots, x(i)) = \begin{cases} x(i) & \text{if } x(j) = x \text{ for } j < i \\ x & \text{otherwise} \end{cases}$$

has an infinite set $J(H)$. Therefore $H \notin [N]$, and thus $M \subseteq N$ is impossible.
Let $F \in M$, $F \notin N$. Let $p_1, p_2 \in J(F)$ be the words with

$$l(p_1) = \min \{ l(q) : q \in J(F) \},$$
$$l(p_2) = \min \{ l(q) : q \in J(F) \setminus \{p_1\}^* \}.$$

We define the functions F_1 and F_2 by

$$\varphi_{F_1}^i(x(1), x(2), \ldots, x(i)) = \begin{cases} \varphi_F^i(x(1), x(2), \ldots, x(i)) & \text{if } p_1 \text{ is is an initial part of } x(1)x(2)\ldots x(i-1) \\ x(i) & \text{otherwise} \end{cases}$$

and

$$\varphi^{i}_{F_2}(x(1),x(2),\dots,x(i)) = \begin{cases} x(i) & \text{if } p_1 \text{ is an initial part of } x(1)x(2)\dots x(i-1) \\ \varphi^{i}_{F}(x(1),x(2),\dots,x(i)) & \text{otherwise.} \end{cases}$$

Obviously, $F_2 \circ F_1 = F$.

<u>Claim 2.</u> $H_2 \circ F \circ H_1 \neq F_1$ and $H_2 \circ F \circ H_1 \neq F_2$ holds for all $H_1, H_2 \in P_k^{\,1}$.

Proof of the claim. By the choice of p_1 and p_2, for each $q \in E_k^{*}$ with $l(q) < l(p_1)$, we have $q \notin I(F)$. Therefore we obtain $q \notin I(F_1) \cup I(F_2)$. If there is a q with $l(q) < l(p_1)$ and $q \notin I(H_2 \circ F \circ H_1)$, then $H_2 \circ F \circ H_1 \neq F_i$ for $i = 1,2$. If such a q does not exist, then for arbitrary p with $l(p) = l(p_1)$ there is an r with $F_{H_1(r)} = F_p$.

Let $I(k,U)$ be the number of all elements of $I(U)$ of length k. Then $I(k,U_1 \circ U_2) \geq I(k,U_i)$ for $i = 1,2$. Thus we have

$$I(l(p_1), F \circ H_1) \geq I(l(p_1), F) \quad \text{and} \quad I(l(p_1), H_2 \circ F \circ H_1) \geq I(l(p_1), F).$$

By the definition of F_2, $p_1 \notin I(F_2)$ holds. Further, p_1 and p_2 are in $J(F)$. By the definition of F_1 we obtain $p_2 \notin I(F_1)$. If $l(p_1) = l(p_2)$, then $I(l(p_1), F_1)$ and $I(l(p_1), F_2)$ are smaller than $I(l(p_1), H_2 \circ F \circ H_1)$. Thus $F_i \neq H_2 \circ F \circ H_1$ for $i = 1,2$.

If $l(p_1) < l(p_2)$, then $I(F)$ contains no word of length $l(p_1)$ with the exception of p_1. As $p_1 \notin I(F_2)$, $I(l(p_1), F_2) = 0$ holds. Hence $I(l(p_1), F_2) < I(l(p_1), F)$. Therefore

$$I(l(p_1),\ H_2 \circ F \circ H_1) > I(l(p_1),\ F_2).$$

Thus $H_2 \circ F \circ H_1 \neq F_2$.

If $l(q) < l(p_1)$, then $q \notin I(H_2 \circ F \circ H_1)$ or $H_2 \circ F \circ H_1 \neq F_1$ as shown above. Hence let $q \notin I(H_1)$. Then, for every word $r \in E_k^{*}$ of length less than or equal to $l(p_1)$, there exists a word $t \in E_k^{*}$ with $H_1(t) = r$. If $H_1(p_1) \neq p_1$, then $H_1(s) = p_1$ for some $s \in E_k^{*}$, $s \neq p_1$, $l(s) = l(p_1)$. Since $p_1 \in I(F)$, we have $s \in I(H_2 \circ F \circ H_1)$, and $s \notin I(F_1)$ holds by $p_1 \neq s$. Therefore $H_2 \circ F \circ H_1 \neq F_1$.

Now let $H_1(p_1) = p_1$ and $p_2 = pr$, where $l(p) = l(p_1)$. Then there is a word q with $H_1(q) = p$ (in the opposite case $H_2 \circ F \circ H_1 \neq F_1$ is shown above). Obviously, p_1 is not a proper initial part of p_2. Therefore $p \neq p_1$ and $q \neq p_1$. This implies $F_1(qs) = ps$ for all $s \in E_k^{*}$. Hence $qs \notin I(F_1)$. If there is no word r_1 with $H_1(qr_1) = pr$, then $H_2 \circ F \circ H_1 \neq F_1$ because in this case there is a word r_2 with

$qr_2 \in I(H_2 \circ F \circ H_1)$. If $H_1(qr_1) = pr$, then $qr_1 \in I(H_2 \circ F \circ H_1)$ by $p_2 \in I(F)$. Therefore $H_2 \circ F \circ H_1 \neq F_1$.
Thus the claim is proved.

Now, let F be an arbitrary function of M. Then the associated functions F_1 and F_2 can be generated from M and, by Claim 2, F is not used in this generation. Therefore $F \in [M \setminus \{F\}]$. This proves that M is not a basis.

Independently, J.Horejs and V.P.Zarovnij (/Ho/, /Za/) showed

<u>Lemma 6.4.</u> The subset G_k of all one-to-one mappings of P_k^1 forms a group $(G_k, \circ)$.

Without proof we note

<u>Lemma 6.5.</u> $\underline{G_k}$ is of type 2, especially it is not finitely generated.

Here, we introduced this group in order to demonstrate that sequential functions can also be used in other fields of mathematics.
In 1902 W.Burnside posed the following group theoretical problem:
Does there exist an infinite finitely generated group such that each element of the group has a finite order [1)] (where the order of an element a is defined as the smallest integer $n > 0$ such that $a^n = e$ and the powers of a are inductively given by $a^1 = a$, $a^{i+1} = a^i \circ a$ for $i > 1$). S.V.Alesin gave the following positive answer.

<u>Lemma 6.6.</u> There are two elements of G_k which generate an infinite subgroup of $\underline{G_k}$ such that each element of this subgroup has a finite order.

Finally, we give some properties of $(P_k^1, \circ)$ with respect to the modified concepts of completeness introduced in the paragraphs 5.1. and 5.2..

<u>Theorem 6.7.</u> i) There is no finitely generated subsemigroup of P_2^1 which is metrically equivalent to P_2^1.

---

1) The first solution of this problem was given in /Go/.
Nowadays the Burnside problem has the following sharper form: Does there exist an infinite finitely generated group such that $a^n = e$ for all elements a of this group and a certain fixed integer $n > 0$. (In the above formulation the order was not bounded.) We refer to /Hal/ and /Ad/.

ii) There is a subsemigroup of $\underline{P_2^1}$ which has a basis and is metrically equivalent to P_2^1.
iii) There is a subsemigroup of $\underline{P_2^1}$ which is metrically equivalent to P_2^1 and of type 2.

Sketch of the proof. i) Let F be a sequential function of P_2^1 and let $t \geq 1$. Then there is an automaton $\mathfrak{A}(F,t) = (E_2, E_2, Z, g, f, z_o)$ such that

$$(*) \quad g(z_o,p) = g(z_o,px) \quad \text{for all} \quad x \in E_2,\ p \in E_2^*,\ l(p) \geq t$$

and

$$\varphi_F^i = \varphi_{F_{\mathfrak{A}(F,t)}}^i \quad \text{for all} \quad i \leq t.$$

For $M \subseteq P_2^1$ we put

$$M|_t = \{F_{\mathfrak{A}(F,t)} : F \in M\}.$$

It can be easily proved (see /Th3/) that $[M]$ is m-equivalent to P_2^1 if and only if, for all $t \geq 1$, $[M|_t]$ contains the set $D(t)$ of all sequential functions of P_2^1 which are induced by automata satisfying the condition $(*)$.
Now suppose that M' is finitely generated and that M' is m-equivalent to P_2^1. Let $\{F_1,F_2,\dots,F_n\}$ be a system of generators for M'. Then $[\{F_1,F_2,\dots,F_n\}|_n] = D(n)$. Therefore $D(n)$ has a basis which consists of m elements with $m \leq n$. This contradicts /Th3/ where it is proved that any basis of $D(n)$ consists of $2n$ elements.
ii) Such an example is given in /Th3/.
iii) Take P_2^1.

In addition, by the results of /Th3/ we have

Lemma 6.8. Let t be an integer, $t \geq 1$. Then
i) there are finitely generated subsemigroups of $\underline{P_2^1}$ which are t-equivalent to P_2^1,
ii) for a given finite set $M \subseteq P_2^1$, it is decidable whether or not $[M]$ is t-equivalent to P_2^1.

A subsemigroup $M \leq P_2^1$ is called a 1-Kleene-set iff, for each regular set $R \leq E_2^*$, there is a sequential function $F \in M$ which accepts R.

Theorem 6.9. i) There is no finitely generated 1-Kleene-set in P_2^1.
ii) There are 1-Kleene-sets of type 2 in P_2^1.

Proof. i) If M is a 1-Kleene-set in $P_2^{\,1}$, then $[M \cup \{F_{(non)}\}] = P_2^{\,1}$. If M is finitely generated, we obtain that $P_2^{\,1}$ is finitely generated, too. This contradicts Theorem 6.2..
ii) $P_2^{\,1}$, $M_{T_0} \cap P_2^{\,1}$, and $M_{T_1} \cap P_2^{\,1}$ are Kleene-sets in $P_2^{\,1}$ and they are of type 2 (this can be proved as in Theorem 6.3.).

Exercises

1. Prove that $M_{T_0} \cap P_k^{\,1}$ is of type 2.
2. Prove that the set of subsemigroups of $\underline{P_2^{\,1}}$ which are metrically equivalent to $P_2^{\,1}$ has the cardinality $\mathfrak{c}$.
3. Prove that the set of 1-Kleene-sets in $P_2^{\,1}$ has the cardinality $\mathfrak{c}$.
4. Show that $M_{T_0} \cap P_2^{\,1}$ is a minimal 1-Kleene-set. Give an example of a minimal 1-Kleene-set in $P_2^{\,1}$ which is different from $M_{T_i} \cap P_2^{\,1}$, $i = 1,2$.

7. FURTHER COMPLETENESS CONCEPTS

In the preceding chapters we used the operations ζ, τ, Δ, ∇, $\times$, and $\circ$, which are motivated by the connections of logical nets. If we realize a logical net by some gates in practice, we have to take into consideration some further aspects, for instance hazards and races. Therefore we have to modify the description of the working mechanism of a net and the operations.
The above operations can only be applied if the input set is the cartesian power of a certain (finite)set and the output set has to be the same set. In the theory of abstract automata the input set and the output set are arbitrary (finite) sets. Hence we have to use modifications, too.
The abstract automaton (or the logical net) is a model for a computation process. The register machines are another model. It needs different operations, again.

7.1. Delayed Functions

In Chapter 3 we have studied the algebra $\underline{P_k'}$ of functions over a finite set (especially E_k). The realization of such functions is done by logical nets which need no storage element $F_{(id;1;0)}$ or $F_{(id;1;1)}$, i.e. by so-called combinational circuits. In the considerations (also concerning P_k) we have assumed that there is no time delay if the signals pass through the gates, i.e. if the gate realizes the function $f \in P_k'^{2}$, then the output signal $f(x_1(t),x_2(t))$ at the moment t depends only on the input signals $x_1(t)$ and $x_2(t)$ at the same time moment t. However, practically in a physical realization of a gate there is a time delay. This delay may sometimes be neglected, but there are a lot of problems concerning hazards, races, etc., where the real delay is very important. In this connection we have to consider delayed functions.

A delayed function is a pair (f, d) where $f \in P_k'$ and $d \in \mathbb{N}$. The interpretation is as follows: The logical net realizes the function f and the output of the net at the time moment t is $f(x_1(t-d),x_2(t-d),\dots,x_n(t-d))$ and depends on the inputs at the time moment $t - d$. For $t \leq d$ we are not interested in the output.
We put

$$Q_k = \{(f, d) : f \in P_k', \ d \in \mathbb{N}\}.$$

The operations τ, ζ, Δ, ∇ can also be given in this case. We define

$$\tau((f,d)) = (\tau f,\ d),$$
$$\zeta((f,d)) = (\zeta f,\ d),$$
$$\Delta((f,d)) = (\Delta f,\ d),$$
$$\nabla((f,d)) = (\nabla f,\ d).$$

The operation $\circ$ is not useful since

$$(f,\ d_1)\circ(g,\ d_2)$$

depends on

$$x_1(t-d_1-d_2),\ x_2(t-d_1-d_2),\ \ldots,\ x_m(t-d_1-d_2),$$
$$x_{m+1}(t-d_1),\ x_{m+2}(t-d_1),\ \ldots,\ x_{n+m-1}(t-d_1).$$

Instead of $\circ$ we shall use the synchronous substitution $\otimes$. For

$$f\in P_k'^{\,n},\quad g_1\in P_k'^{\,m_1},\quad g_2\in P_k'^{\,m_2},\ \ldots,\ g_n\in P_k'^{\,m_n}$$

and integers

$$d,\ d_1,\ d_2,\ \ldots,\ d_n\geq 0$$

we define $(f,d)\otimes((g_1,d_1),(g_2,d_2),\ldots,g_n,d_n))$ if and only if $d_1 = d_2 = \ldots = d_n$ holds, and then we put

$$(f,d)\otimes((g_1,d_1),(g_2,d_n),\ldots,(g_n,d_1)) = (h,\ d+d_1)$$

where

$$h(\underline{x}) = f(g_1(\underline{x}_1),g_2(\underline{x}_2),\ldots,g_n(\underline{x}_n)),$$

and $\underline{x} = (x_1,x_2,\ldots,x_{m_1+m_2+\ldots+m_n})$,

$$\underline{x}_i = (x_{m_1+\ldots+m_{i-1}+1},\ x_{m_1+\ldots+m_{i-1}+1},\ \ldots,\ x_{m_1+\ldots+m_i})\ \text{for}\ 1\leq i\leq n.$$

are the tupels of variables of h, g_1, $g_2,\ldots,$ g_n, respectively. Let

$$\underline{Q_k} = (Q_k;\ \tau,\ \zeta,\ \Delta,\ \nabla,\ \otimes).$$

By $[M]_d$ we denote the closure of a set $M\subseteq Q_k$ in $\underline{Q_k}$. For any $M\subseteq Q_k$, we put

$$M^{+r} = \{f\ :\ (f,r)\in M\}$$

and

$$M^+ = \{f : (f,d) \in M \text{ for some } d \in \mathbb{N}\} = \bigcup_{r \geq 0} M^{+r} .$$

With respect to the importance of the delay we can now define the following completeness concepts for $\underline{Q_k}$.

i) A set $M \subseteq Q_k$ is called d_1-complete iff

$$[M]_d = Q_k ,$$

i.e. any function of P_k' can be realized with any delay.

ii) A set $M \subseteq Q_k$ is called d_2-complete iff

$$[M]_d{}^+ = P_k' ,$$

i.e. for any function there is a realization with a certain delay.

iii) A set $M \subseteq Q_k$ is called d_3-complete iff

$$[M]_d{}^{+r} = P_k' \quad \text{for some } r \in \mathbb{N}.$$

iv) A set $M \subseteq Q_k$ is called $d(r)$-complete iff

$$[M]_d{}^{+r} = P_k' ,$$

i.e. any function can be realized with a fixed delay r.

We now discuss the completeness problems connected with these concepts.

Theorem 7.1. $M \subseteq Q_k$ is d_1-complete if and only if it satisfies the following conditions:

i) $[M^{+0}]_{\underline{P_k'}} = P_k'$,

ii) $(f,1) \in M$ for some nonconstant function $f \in P_k'$.

Proof. $\Rightarrow$) i) holds by

$$[M]_d{}^{+0} = [M^{+0}]_d = [M^{+0}]_{\underline{P_k'}} ,$$

and ii) holds since in the opposite case $[M]_d{}^{+1}$ is contained in the set of constant functions of P_k'.

$\Leftarrow$) The function f essentially depends at least on one, say the first variable. Then there are values $a, b, a_2, a_3, \ldots, a_n$ such that

$$c = f(a,a_2,a_3,\dots,a_n) \neq f(b,a_2,a_3,\dots,a_n) = d .$$

Now we consider the functions $h_i \in P_k'^{\,1}$, $h_i' \in P_k'^{\,1}$, $0 \le i \le k-1$, and $t \in P_k'^{\,k}$ defined by

$$h_i(x) = \begin{cases} c & \text{if } x = i \\ d & \text{otherwise,} \end{cases}$$

$$h_i'(x) = \begin{cases} a & \text{if } x = i \\ b & \text{otherwise,} \end{cases}$$

$$t(x_0,x_1,\dots,x_{k-1}) = \begin{cases} i & \text{if } x_i = c \text{ and } x_j = d \text{ for } j \neq i \\ 0 & \text{otherwise.} \end{cases}$$

Then we have

$$(h_i,1) = (f,1) \otimes ((h_i',0),(k_{a_2},0),(k_{a_3},0),\dots,(k_{a_n},0)) \quad \text{for } i \in E_k,$$

$$(id,1) = (t,0) \otimes ((h_0,1),(h_1,0),\dots,(h_{k-1},0)),$$

and for an arbitrary delayed function $(g,d) \in Q_k$ we obtain

$$(g,d) = (id,1) \otimes ((id,1) \otimes (\dots \otimes ((id,1) \otimes ((g,0)))\dots)) .$$

Thus $Q_k = [M]_d$.

Corollary 7.2. i) $\underline{Q_k}$ is finitely generated.

ii) Any system of generators of $\underline{Q_k}$ contains at least two elements.

By Theorem 7.1., we have immediately the following completeness criterion.

Theorem 7.3. i) $M \subseteq Q_k$ is d_1-complete if and only if it is not contained in any maximal subalgebra of $\underline{Q_k}$.

ii) The maximal subalgebras of $\underline{Q_k}$ have the following carriers:

$$D_N = \{(f,d) : f \in P_k',\ d \ge 1\} \cup \{(f,0) : f \in N\},$$

where $\underline{N}$ is a maximal subalgebra of $\underline{P_k'}$,

$$D_1 = \{(f,d) : f \in P_k',\ d \neq 1\} \cup \{(f,1) : f \text{ is a constant mapping}\}.$$

Theorem 7.4. The d_1-completeness of a finite subset of Q_k is decidable.

Let $M \subseteq Q_k^{+0}$. Then M is d_2-complete in $\underline{Q_k}$ if and only if M^+ is complete in $\underline{P_k'}$. Hence the completeness in $\underline{P_k'}$ can be regarded as a special case of the d_2-completeness. Especially, $\{(sh,0)\}$ is d_2-complete in contrast to Corollary 7.2.ii) concerning d_1-completeness.

<u>Lemma 7.5.</u> The set $\{(f,d)\}$ is d_2-complete if and only if $d = 0$ and $[\{f\}]_{\underline{P_k'}} = P_k'$.

<u>Proof.</u> For simplicity we give the proof only for $k = 2$.
$\Rightarrow$) Let $d = 0$. Then f has to generate P_k' in $\underline{P_k'}$.
Let $d \geq 1$. Since we can only construct functions (h,t) where d is a divisor of t, we can assume that $d = 1$. Let

$$M = [\{(f,1)\}]_d .$$

By Lemma 3.6., M^{+1} contains only functions h with

$$h(0,0,\ldots,0) = 1, \quad h(1,1,\ldots,1) = 0$$

because h is obtained from f by applications of $\tau, \zeta, \Delta, \nabla$. Further, M^{+2} contains only functions g with

$$g(0,0,\ldots,0) = 0, \quad g(1,1,\ldots,1) = 1$$

since there are functions $h, h_1, h_2, \ldots, h_n \in M^{+1}$ such that

$$g(x_1,x_2,\ldots,x_m) = h(h_1(x_1,x_2,\ldots,x_m),\ldots,h_n(x_1,x_2,\ldots,x_m)).$$

Continuing this process we obtain that, for $t \geq 1$,

$$g' \in M^{+2t} \text{ implies } g'(0,0,\ldots,0) = 0,\ g'(1,1,\ldots,1) = 1,$$

$$h' \in M^{+(2t-1)} \text{ implies } h'(0,0,\ldots,0) = 1,\ h'(1,1,\ldots,1) = 0.$$

Therefore $k_0 \notin M^+$, i.e. $\{(f,1)\}$ is not d_2-complete.
$\Leftarrow$) The converse direction is obvious.

The validity of the statements of Lemma 3.3. also depends essentially on the delays. The following assertions hold in $\underline{Q_2}$:
- $\{(et,2), (id,2), (non,1), (k_0,0), (k_1,0)\}$ is not d_2-complete,
- $\{(et,1), (id,1), (non,1), (k_0,1), (k_1,1)\}$ is d_2-complete,
- $\{(et,2), (non,1)\}$ is not d_2-complete,
- $\{(et,1), (non,1)\}$ is d_2-complete.

We give the following criterion for d_2-completeness.

Theorem 7.6. $M \subseteq Q_k$ is d_2-complete if and only if $(id,t) \in [M]_d$ and $(f_i, d_i t) \in M_d$, $1 \le i \le s$, for some integers $t, d_1, d_2, \dots, d_s \in \mathbb{N}$ and a set $\{f_1, f_2, \dots, f_s\} \in P'_k$ which is complete in $\underline{P'_k}$.

Proof. $\Rightarrow$) Let $f \in P'^{3}_k$ be defined by

$$f(x_1,x_2,x_3) = \begin{cases} sh(x_1,x_2) & \text{if } x_3 = 1 \\ x_3 & \text{otherwise.} \end{cases}$$

Since M is d_2-complete, we have

$$(id,t_1) \in [M]_d, \quad (k_o,t_2) \in [M]_d, \quad (k_1,t_3) \in [M]_d,$$

$$(f, t_4) \in [M]_d, \quad (sh,t_5) \in [M]_d$$

for some integers $t_1,t_2,t_3,t_4,t_5 \ge 0$. If $t_5 = 0$, then $(id,0) \in [M]_d$, and the statement is proved. If $t_5 \ne 0$, then $(id, kt_5) \in [M]_d$ by

$$cyc(x) = sh(x,x) \quad \text{and} \quad cyc^k = id.$$

Hence we can assume that $t_1 \ne 0$, and therefore $t_2 \ne 0$, $t_3 \ne 0$, and $t_4 \ne 0$, too. Let $t = t_1 t_2 t_3$. It is easy to prove that

$$(id,t), (k_o,t), (k_1,t) \in [M]_d .$$

Therefore

$$(sh, t+t_4) \in [M]_d \quad \text{and} \quad (id, t+t_4) \in [M]_d$$

because

$$sh(x_1,x_2) = f(x_1,x_2,k_1(x_1)),$$

$$id(x) = f(k_o(x),k_o(x),x).$$

$\Leftarrow$) Since $(id,t) \in [M]_d$, we have $(id,nt) \in [M]_d$ for $n = 1,2,\dots$. Let $(g_1,rt) \in [M]_d$ and $(g_2,st) \in [M]_d$. Then

$$(g_2 \circ g_1, (r+s)t) = (g_2,st) \otimes ((g_1,rt),(id,rt),\dots,(id,rt)) \in [M]_d.$$

Thus

$$M^+ \supseteq [\{f_1,f_2,\dots,f_s\}]_{\underline{P'_k}} = P'_k .$$

Obviously, Theorem 7.6. does not solve the completeness problem since it uses the closure $[M]_d$ which is unknown in general.

$M \subseteq Q_k$ is called d_2-precomplete if M is not d_2-complete and $M \cup \{(f,d)\}$ is d_2-complete for any $(f,d) \notin M$.

Theorem 7.7. i) A subset of Q_k is d_2-complete if and only if it is not contained in any d_2-precomplete set of Q_k.
ii) The set of d_2-precomplete sets of Q_k is infinitely countable.

In /Ku1/ V.B.Kudrjavcev has determined all d_2-precomplete sets in Q_2. For $k \geq 3$, in /HN/ a description of a set $\mathfrak{M}$ is given where $\mathfrak{M}$ contains all d_2-precomplete sets. The infinity of the set of d_2-precomplete sets arises since there is no bound for the delays of the functions in M. However, if M is finite, there is such a bound, and we can find a finite set of d_2-precomplete sets which give a criterion for the completeness of M.
Instead of the long proof of Theorem 7.7. we present an analogous solution of the d_2-completeness problem for the special case that $M = M^{+d}$ for some $d \geq 1$. Notice that $d = 0$ is considered in Chapter 3, and evidently we can suppose that $d = 1$.

We say that a set $M \subseteq P_k'$ is uniformly precomplete (u-precomplete) if and only if

i) $M' = \{(f,1) : f \in M\}$ is not d_2-complete,
ii) for any function $g \in P_k' \setminus M$, $M' \cup \{(g,1)\}$ is d_2-complete.

The characterization of the u-precomplete sets, which will be given below, is closely related to the description of d_2-precomplete sets in /HN/.

Theorem 7.8. Let $M \subseteq P_k'$ and $M' = \{(f,1) : f \in M\}$. Then

i) M' is d_2-complete if and only if M is not contained in any uniformly precomplete set of P_k',
ii) the number of uniformly precomplete sets in P_k' is finite,
iii) if M is finite, then the d_2-completeness of M' is decidable.

Proof. We prove some claims which are of interest themselves.

Claim 1. $M \subseteq N(k)$ if and only if $[M']_d^{+n} \subseteq N(k)$ for some $n \geq 1$. (For the definition of $N(k)$ we refer to Chapter 3.)

Proof of claim 1. $\Rightarrow$) If $M \subseteq N(k)$, then

$$[M']_d^{+n} \subseteq [M]_{P_k'} \subseteq N(k).$$

$\Leftarrow$) Assume $M \nsubseteq N(k)$. We prove $[M']_d^{+n} \nsubseteq N(k)$ for all $n \geq 1$ by induction on n.

Evidently, $[M']_d^{+1} \nsubseteq N(k)$.

Let $(f,n) \in [M']_d$, $f \in P_k'^p$, and $(g,1) \in [M']_d$, $g \in P_k'^q$. Then $(h,n+1) \in [M']_d$ where

$$h(x_1,x_2,\dots,x_{pq}) =$$
$$= f(g(x_1,\dots,x_q),g(x_{q+1},\dots,x_{2q}),\dots,g(x_{(p-1)q+1},\dots,x_{pq})).$$

We show that $f, g \notin N(k)$ implies $h \notin N(k)$.

Case 1. $k = 2$. Suppose

$$h \in N(2) = L.$$

Then

$$h(x_1,x_2,\dots,x_{pq}) = a_0 + a_1x_1 + a_2x_2 + \dots + a_{pq}x_{pq} \mod 2.$$

Since f and g are not constants, h essentially depends at least on one variable, say x_1. Further

$$f(y,g(0,\dots,0),g(0,\dots,0),\dots,g(0,\dots,0)) = cy + d \mod 2$$

for some $c, d \in E_2$. Hence

$$a_0 + a_1x_1 + a_2x_2 + \dots + a_qx_q \mod 2$$
$$= h(x_1,x_2,\dots,x_q,0,0,\dots,0)$$
$$= f(g(x_1,x_2,\dots,x_q),g(0,0,\dots 0),\dots,g(0,0,\dots,0))$$
$$= cg(x_1,x_2,\dots,x_q) + d \mod 2.$$

Since $a_1 = 1$, we have $c = 1$, and thus

$$g(x_1,x_2,\dots,x_q) = (d+a_0) + a_1x_1 + a_2x_2 + \dots + a_qx_q .$$

This contradicts $g \notin N(2)$.

Case 2. $k \geq 3$. Since $f, g \notin N(k)$, f and g are surjective. Hence h is surjective, too. If $h \in N(k)$, then h has to depend exactly on one variable, say x_1. By the surjectivity of g, for any b, there are values

$$a_{b1}, a_{b2}, \dots, a_{bq}$$

such that

$$g(a_{b1},a_{b2},\dots,a_{bq}) = b.$$

Then, for any $b_1,b_2,\dots,b_p$, we have

$f(b_1,b_2,\dots,b_p)$

$= f(g(a_{b_1 1},a_{b_1 2},\dots,a_{b_1 q}),\dots,g(a_{b_p 1},a_{b_p 2},\dots,a_{b_p q}))$

$= h(a_{b_1 1},a_{b_1 2},\dots,a_{b_1 q},\dots,a_{b_p 1},a_{b_p 2},\dots,a_{b_p q})$.

The last value depends only on $a_{b_1 1}$. Thus f depends only on b_1. This implies $f \in N(k)$ in contradiction to our assumption.
Claim 1 is proved.

Let $S, S' \subseteq P_k'^{1}$. We define $f \circledast (g_1,g_2,\dots,g_n)$ by

$$(f \circledast (g_1,g_2,\dots,g_n))(x) = f(g_1(x),g_2(x),\dots,g_n(x))$$

and put

$$F(S,S') = \{f : f \circledast (g_1,g_2,\dots,g_n) \in S' \text{ for all } g_1,g_2,\dots,g_n \in S\} .$$

By definition, we have $F(S,S) = F(S)$ ($F(S)$ is defined in Chapter 3). For any sequence $S_o,S_1,\dots,S_n$ of subsets of $P_k'^{1}$ with $S_o = S_n$ we put

$$F(S_o,S_1,\dots,S_n) = \bigcap_{i=1}^{n} F(S_{i-1},S_i).$$

A sequence $S_o,S_1,\dots,S_m$ of subsets of $P_k'^{1}$ is called a normal sequence iff the following conditions are satisfied:

i) S_o is a proper subsemigroup of $P_k'^{1}$,

ii) $S_o = S_n$

iii) $1 \le i < j \le n$ implies $S_i \nsubseteq S_j$.

Claim 2. Let $M \subseteq P_k'$, $n \ge 1$, and let S be a proper subsemigroup of $P_k'^{1}$. Then $[M']_d^{+n} \subseteq F(S)$ if and only if $M \subseteq F(S_o,S_1,\dots,S_n)$ for a sequence $S_o,S_1,\dots,S_n$ of subsets of $P_k'^{1}$ with $S_o = S_n = S$.

Proof of claim 2. $\Rightarrow$) Let $[M']_d^{+n} \subseteq F(S)$. Then we put

$$S_o' = S$$

and

$$S_i' = \{f \circledast (g_1,g_2,\dots,g_n) : f \in [M']_d^{+i},\ g_1,g_2,\dots,g_n \in S\} .$$

By this definition and $[M']_d^{+n} \subseteq F(S)$, we have $S_n' \subseteq S$. We put

$$S_i' = S_i \quad \text{for } 0 \le i \le n-1 \quad \text{and} \quad S_n = S.$$

Then

$$M \subseteq F(S'_{i-1}, S'_i) \subseteq F(S_{i-1}, S_i) \quad \text{for} \quad 1 \le i \le n.$$

Thus

$$M \subseteq F(S_o, S_1, \dots, S_n).$$

$\Leftarrow$) Let $M \subseteq F(S_o, S_1, \dots, S_n)$, where $S_o = S_n = S$. We have the relation

$$\{f \circledast (g_1, g_2, \dots, g_n) : f \in [M']_d^{+1}, \quad g_1, g_2, \dots, g_n \in S_o\} \subseteq S_1,$$

and by induction we can show that

$$\{f \circledast (g_1, g_2, \dots, g_n) : f \in [M']_d^{+i}, \; g_1, g_2, \dots, g_n \in S_o\} \subseteq S_i.$$

Since $S_n = S_o$, we obtain

$$[M']_d^{+n} \subseteq F(S,S) = F(S).$$

Claim 3. If $M \subseteq F(S_o, S_1, \dots, S_n)$ for some sequence $S_o, S_1, \dots, S_n$, where S_o is a proper subsemigroup of $P_k'^{1}$ and $S_o = S_n$, then $M \subseteq F(S'_o, S'_1, \dots, S'_m)$ for some normal sequence $S'_o, S'_1, \dots, S'_m$.
Proof of claim 3. If $S_i \subseteq S_j$ for some i, j, $1 \le i < j \le n$, then

$$S_o, S_1, \dots, S_{i-1}, S_j, S_{j+1}, \dots, S_n$$

is also a sequence which satisfies

$$M \subseteq F(S_o, S_1, \dots, S_{i-1}, S_j, S_{j+1}, \dots, S_n).$$

Continuing this process we obtain a normal sequence.
For $a, b \in E_k$, $a \neq b$, we put

$$K(a,b) = \{f : f \in P'_k, \; f(a,a,\dots,a) = f(b,b,\dots,b)\}.$$

Evidently,

$$[K(a,b)']_d^{+} = K(a,b).$$

Claim 4. Let $M \subseteq P'_k$. M' is d_2-complete if and only if it satisfies the following conditions:

i) for any $n \ge 1$, $[M']_d^{+n}$ is complete in $\underline{P'_k}$,

ii) for any $a, b \in E_k$, $a \neq b$, $M \not\subseteq K(a,b)$.

Proof of claim 4. $\Rightarrow$) If M' is d_2-complete, then ii) is obvious. Let f be the function of the proof of Theorem 7.6. . Since M' is

d_2-complete, we have

$$f\in[M']_d^{+r},\quad id\in[M']_d^{+s},\quad k_o\in[M']_d^{+t},\quad k_1\in[M']_d^{+u}$$

for some r, s, t, u > 0. As in the proof of Theorem 7.6. we can show that

$$sh,\ id\in[M']_d^{+qnm} \quad \text{for some } q \text{ and all } n,\ m\geq 1.$$

Thus

$$\left[[M']_d^{+n}\right]_{\underline{P'_k}} \supseteq [\{sh,\ id\}]_{\underline{P'_k}} = P'_k.$$

$\Leftarrow$) We put

$$R_n = [M']_d^{+n}\cap P_k'^{1}.$$

Then there are integers p,q such that $p<q$ and $R_p = R_q$. Let $S = R_p$. Then $S\subseteq[M']_d^{+p}$ and as in the proof of claim 2 we can prove that $[M']_d^{+(q-p)}\subseteq F(S)$. Therefore $F(S) = P'_k$ by i).
We say that $h\in P_k'^{1}$ separates a and b, $a\neq b$, if $h(a)\neq h(b)$.
By ii) there is a function $f\in M$ such that g given by

$$g(x) = f(x,x,\dots,x)$$

separates a and b. Again, the elements g(a) and g(b) can be separated by a function g'. Then $g'\circ g\in[M']_d^{+2}$ and $g'\circ g$ separates a and b. By induction, we have a function $h_{a,b}\in[M']_d^{+p}$ which separates a and b.
There is a one-to-one mapping φ of $\{1,2,\dots,k^2-k\}$ onto $\{(a,b) : a,b\in E_k,\ a\neq b\}$. If $(a,b) = \varphi(i)$, we put $h_i = h_{a,b}$.
Further we define $v\in P_k'^{k^2-k}$ by

$$v(x_1,x_2,\dots,x_{k^2-k}) = \begin{cases} a & \text{if } x_i = h_i(a) \text{ for } i = 1,2,\dots,k^2-k \\ 0 & \text{otherwise.}\end{cases}$$

Since $F(S) = P'_k$, we have $v\in F(S)$. This implies $id\in[M']_d^{+p}$, because

$$id = v\circledcirc(h_1,h_2,\dots,h_{k^2-k}).$$

Hence

$$[M']_d^{+}\supseteq\bigcup_{n\geq 1}[M']_d^{+pn}\supseteq[M']_d^{+p}\supseteq[M]_{\underline{P'_k}} = P'_k .$$

Claim 5. M' is d_2-complete if and only if

i) $M \nsubseteq K(a,b)$ for all $a, b \in E_k$, $a \neq b$,

ii) $M \nsubseteq N(k)$,

iii) $M \nsubseteq F(S_0,S_1,\dots,S_m)$ for any normal sequence $S_0,S_1,\dots,S_m$.

Proof of claim 5. $\Rightarrow$) Suppose M' is d_2-complete. Then i) holds by Claim 4 and $[M']_d^{+n}$ is complete for any $n \geq 1$. Thus $[M']_d^{+n} \nsubseteq N(k)$ since N(k) is a maximal subalgebra of P_k'. By Claim 1, we have $M \nsubseteq N(k)$. If $M \subseteq F(S_0,S_1,\dots,S_m)$ for some normal sequence $S_0,\dots,S_m$, then $[M']_d^{+m} \subseteq F(S)$ for some proper subsemigroup of $P_k'^{\,1}$ by Claim 2. Hence $[M']_d^{+m}$ is not complete in P_k'. This proves that iii) also holds.

$\Leftarrow$) Assume M is not d_2-complete. Then $M \subseteq K(a,b)$ for some $a,b \in E_k$ or $[M']_d^{+n}$ is not complete in P_k' for some n by Claim 4. In the second case we have $[M']_d^{+n} \subseteq F(S)$ for some proper subsemigroup S of $P_k'^{\,1}$ or $[M']_d^{+n} \subseteq N(k)$ by the proof of Theorem 3.4.. By claim 2 and Claim 3, $[M']_d^{+n} \subseteq F(S)$ implies $M \subseteq F(S_0,S_1,\dots,S_m)$ for some normal sequence $S_0,S_1,\dots,S_m$. Therefore the d_2-incompleteness of M' implies that at least one of the properties i), ii), iii) is not satisfied.

Claim 6. Let M be u-precomplete. Then

$M = K(a,b)$ for some $a,b \in E_k$, $a \neq b$,

or $M = N(k)$,

or $M = F(S_0,S_1,\dots,S_m)$ for some normal sequence $S_0,S_1,\dots,S_m$.

Proof of claim 6. Suppose M is u-precomplete. Then M' is not d_2-complete. Therefore $M \subseteq K(a,b)$ or $M \subseteq N(k)$ or $M \subseteq F(S_0,S_1,\dots,S_m)$ If the proper containment holds, we have a function $f \notin M$ such that $[M \cup \{f\}]$ is also contained in such a set. Therefore $M' \cup \{(f,1)\}$ is not d_2-complete.

Now the theorem follows easily.

Theorem 7.9. The d(r)-completeness, $r \geq 1$, and d_3-completeness of a finite set contained in Q_2 is decidable.

As the proof is quite long, we give only the idea of the proof and refer to /Bi1/, /BK1/, /BK2/ for details. Again, we construct all functions which depend on two variables and have a delay $d \leq r$. Then M is d(r)-complete if and only if $[M]_d^{+r}$ contains all functions which depend on two variables. The proof of the latter fact depends essentially on $[M]_d^{+0}$; **the discussion of 11 cases is necessary.** If M is d_3-complete, then $[M]_d^{+r} = P_2'$ for some $r \geq 0$. It can be shown that $r \leq m^3$ holds where m denotes the maximal delay of the elements of M.

7.2. The Ceitlin Algebra

In connection with the mappings of register computations Ceitlin has given the following modification of the algebra $\underline{P_k'}$.
For $f \in P_k'^n$, $g \in P_k'^m$, we define $f \square g$ by

$$(f \square g)(x_1, x_2, \ldots, x_{mn})$$
$$= f(g(x_1, x_2, \ldots, x_m), g(x_{m+1}, x_{m+2}, \ldots, x_{2m}), \ldots, g(x_{(n-1)m+1}, \ldots, x_{mn}))$$

and put

$$\underline{W_k} = (P_k'; \tau, \zeta, \Delta, \nabla, \square).$$

By $[M]_w$ the closure of M in $\underline{W_k}$ is denoted. Using $\square$ and identifications we can generate the function given by

$$f(g(x_1, x_2, \ldots, x_m), g(x_2, x_3, \ldots, x_{m+1}), \ldots, g(x_n, x_{n+1}, \ldots, x_{n+m-1}))$$

which models the computation in an infinite register machine (see/BC/). We put

$$V_0 = \{f : f(x,x,\ldots,x) = 0\} \cup \{f : f(x,x,\ldots,x) = 1\},$$

$$V_1 = \{f : f(x,x,\ldots,x) = x\} \cup V_0,$$

$$V_2 = \{f : f(x,x,\ldots,x) = x\} \cup \{f : f(x,x,\ldots,x) = \mathrm{non}(x)\},$$

$$V_3 = [P_2'^0]_{\underline{P_2'}} \cup V_2$$

$$V_4 = \{f : f \in \mathcal{M} \text{ or } \mathrm{non} \circ f \in \mathcal{M}\} \cup V_0;$$

$$V_5 = \{f : f \in S\} \cup V_0.$$

($\mathcal{M}$ and S are defined in Chapter 3.) It is easy to prove that $\underline{V_0}, \underline{V_1}, \underline{V_2}, \underline{V_3}, \underline{V_4}, \underline{V_5}$ are subalgebras of $\underline{W_2}$.

Theorem 7.10. i) $\underline{W_2}$ is finitely generated.
ii) There is no single function which generates $\underline{W_2}$.

Proof. i) For $n \geq 1$, we define the functions et_n, l_n, l'_n by

$$et_n(x_1,x_2,\ldots,x_n) = \max(x_1,x_2,\ldots,x_n),$$

$$l_n(x_1,x_2,\ldots,x_n) = x_1 + x_2 + \ldots + x_n \mod 2 ,$$

$$l'_n(x_1,x_2,\ldots,x_n) = x_1 + x_2 + \ldots + x_n + 1 \mod 2 .$$

We prove that et_2, l_2, l'_3 is a system of generators for $\underline{W_2}$. Obviously,

$$et_2 \Box et_n = et_{2n} \quad \text{for } n \geq 1.$$

By identifications, we have $et_m \in [\{et_2\}]_W$ for any $m \geq 1$. Further

$$l'_1(x) = l'_3(x,x,x),$$

$$l_2 \Box l_n = l_{2n}, \quad l'_3 \Box l_n = l'_{3n},$$

$$l'_1 \Box l_n = l'_n, \quad l'_1 \Box l'_n = l_n,$$

and therefore

$$\{l_n : n \geq 1\} \cup \{l'_n : n \geq 1\} \subseteq [\{l_2, l'_3\}]_W.$$

Furthermore, we have

$$(l_n \Box et_m)(x_1,x_2,\ldots,x_{mn})$$

$$= x_1x_2\ldots x_m + x_{m+1}x_{m+2}\ldots x_{2m} + \ldots + x_{(n-1)m+1}x_{(n-1)m+2}\ldots x_{nm} \mod 2$$

and

$$(l'_n \Box et_m)(x_1,x_2,\ldots,x_{mn})$$

$$= x_1x_2\ldots x_m + x_{m+1}x_{m+2}\ldots x_{2m} + \ldots + x_{(n-1)m+1}x_{(n-1)m+2}\ldots x_{nm} + 1 \mod 2$$

By identifications of some variables, we can obtain any function of P'_2 by the representation as a polynomial.

ii) The subalgebra $\underline{V_2}$ has the following property: If $f \notin V_2$, then $\alpha f \notin V_2$ for $\alpha \in \{\tau, \zeta, \Delta, \nabla\}$, and if $f \notin V_2$ or $g \notin V_2$, then $f \Box g \notin V_2$. This can be proved easily by the discussion of all possible cases.

Let $h \in P'_2$. If $h \in V_2$, then $[\{h\}]_W \subseteq V_2$. If $h \notin V_2$, then $f \notin V_2$ for any $f \in [\{h\}]_W$. In both cases, $[\{h\}]_W \neq W_2$.

Theorem 7.11. $M \subseteq P_2'$ is complete in W_2 if and only if M is not contained in the following sets: V_1, V_3, V_4, V_5.

Proof. $\Leftarrow$) This follows since $\underline{V_1}$, $\underline{V_3}$, $\underline{V_4}$, $\underline{V_5}$ are proper subalgebras.

$\Rightarrow$) Let

$$f_1 \notin V_1, \quad f_2 \notin V_5, \quad f_3 \notin V_4, \quad f_4 \notin V_3,$$

$$f_1 \in P_2'^m, \quad f_2 \in P_2'^n, \quad f_3 \in P_2'^r, \quad f_4 \in P_2'^s.$$

Then $f_1(x,x,\ldots,x) = \mathrm{non}(x)$, i.e. $\mathrm{non} \in [\{f_1,f_2,f_3,f_4\}]_w$. Further $f_2(x,x,\ldots,x) = x$ or $f_2(x,x,\ldots,x) = \mathrm{non}(x)$. In the second case let $g_2 = \mathrm{non} \,\square\, f_2$. Evidently, $g_2 \notin V_5$ and $g_2 \in [\{f_1,f_2,f_3,f_4\}]_w$, too. Thus we can assume without loss of generality that f_2 satisfies $f_2(x,x,\ldots,x) = x$.

By the same arguments, we can assume that $f_3(x,x,\ldots,x) = x$ and $f_4(x,x,\ldots,x) = 0$.

Let $a_1,a_2,\ldots,a_n$ be the arguments such that

$$f_2(a_1,a_2,\ldots,a_n) = f_2(\mathrm{non}(a_1),\mathrm{non}(a_2),\ldots,\mathrm{non}(a_n)) .$$

If we identify the variables with $a_i = 0$ and the variables with $a_j = 1$, then we obtain a function $h_2 \in P_k'^2$ such that

$$h_2 = \begin{cases} \mathrm{et} & \text{if } f_2(a_1,a_2,\ldots,a_n) = 0 \\ \mathrm{vel} & \text{if } f_2(a_1,a_2,\ldots,a_n) = 1 . \end{cases}$$

Using non and de Morgan's formulae we conclude that

$$\{\mathrm{et}, \mathrm{vel}\} \subseteq [\{f_1,f_2,f_3,f_4\}]_w .$$

Hence $\varphi \in [\{f_1,f_2,f_3,f_4\}]_w$ where

$$\varphi(x_1,x_2,\ldots,x_9) = \mathrm{vel}(\mathrm{et}(x_1,x_2,x_3),\mathrm{et}(x_4,x_5,x_6),\mathrm{et}(x_7,x_8,x_9)).$$

Let $b_1,b_2,\ldots,b_{i-1},b_{i+1},b_{i+2},\ldots,b_r$ be values such that

$$f_3(b_1,b_2,\ldots,b_{i-1}, x, b_{i+1},b_{i+2},\ldots,b_r) = \mathrm{non}(x).$$

Using the same identifications as in the generation of h_2, we obtain a function $h_3 \in P_k'^3$ with

$$h_3(0,0,0) = 0, \quad h_3(1,1,1) = 1, \quad h_3(0,1,0) = 1, \quad h_3(0,1,1) = 0.$$

As

$$h_3(et(x,y,z),vel(x,y,z),vel(et(x,y),et(x,z),et(y,z))) = x + y + z \mod 2,$$

we can generate the function l_3 from $h_3 \square \varphi$ by identification of variables. Since $l_3' = non \square l_3$, we have

$$l_3' \in [\{f_1,f_2,f_3,f_4\}]_W .$$

Since f_4 is not a constant, there are $c_1,c_2,\ldots,c_s \in E_2$ such that

$$f_4(c_1,c_2,\ldots,c_s) = 1.$$

Again, by identifications, we construct h_4 such that

$$h_4(x,y) = \begin{cases} x + y \mod 2 & \text{if } f_4(non(c_1),\ldots,non(c_s)) = 1 \\ et(non(x),y) & \text{otherwise.} \end{cases}$$

Since

$$vel(et(non(x),y),et(non(x),y)) = x + y \mod 2,$$

we can generate l_2 from h_4 and vel in the second case, too.
Therefore

$$l_2 \in [\{f_1,f_2,f_3,f_4\}]_W .$$

Thus we have

$$P_2' = [\{et, l_2, l_3'\}]_W \subseteq [\{f_1,f_2,f_3,f_4\}]_W .$$

<u>Corollary 7.12.</u> $\underline{W_2}$ has exactly the following four maximal subalgebras $\underline{V_1}$, $\underline{V_3}$, $\underline{V_4}$, and $\underline{V_5}$.

By theorem 7.11., we also have immediately

<u>Theorem 7.13.</u> It is decidable whether or not a finite set contained in P_2' is complete in $\underline{W_2}$.

7.3. Completeness in Abstract Automata Theory

We need some additional concepts of automata theory.
Let $\mathfrak{A} = (X, Y, Z, g, f)$ be an automaton without initial state, i.e. there is no distinguished state in which the automaton starts.
$\mathfrak{B} = (X, Y, Z', g', f')$ is called a Z-subautomaton of $\mathfrak{A}$ iff $Z' \subseteq Z$ and g' and f' are the restrictions of g and f on $Z' \times X$.
The automata $\mathfrak{A} = (X, Y, Z, g, f)$ and $\mathfrak{B} = (X', Y', Z', g', f')$ are called isomorphic iff there are bijective mappings

$$\alpha_1 : X \rightarrow X', \quad \alpha_2 : Y \rightarrow Y', \quad \alpha_3 : Z \rightarrow Z'$$

such that, for all $x \in X$, $z \in Z$,

$$\alpha_3(g(z,x)) = g'(\alpha_3(z), \alpha_1(x)),$$

$$\alpha_2(f(z,x)) = f'(\alpha_3(z), \alpha_1(x)).$$

In some cases, it is sufficient to consider the behaviour of states of an automaton (for instance with respect to its acceptance power, see /St/,I,§5). Therefore we can regard automata $\mathfrak{A} = (X, Z, g)$ without outputs in this connection.
Let $\mathfrak{A}_1, \mathfrak{A}_2, \ldots, \mathfrak{A}_n$ be automata without initial states. Let

$$\mathfrak{A}_i = (X_i, Y_i, Z_i, g_i, f_i), \quad i = 1,2,\ldots,n,$$

and let X and Y be arbitrary nonempty sets. Furthermore, let

$$\varphi : Z_1 \times Z_2 \times \ldots \times Z_n \times X \longrightarrow X_1 \times X_2 \times \ldots \times X_n ,$$

$$\psi : Z_1 \times Z_2 \times \ldots \times Z_n \times X \longrightarrow Y$$

be arbitrary functions. Then we define the product of $\mathfrak{A}_1, \mathfrak{A}_2, \ldots, \mathfrak{A}_n$ with respect to φ and ψ as the automaton

$$\mathfrak{A} = (X, Y, Z_1 \times Z_2 \times \ldots \times Z_n, g, f)$$

where

$$f((z_1,z_2,\ldots,z_n),x) = \psi(z_1,z_2,\ldots,z_n,x),$$
$$g((z_1,z_2,\ldots,z_n),x) = (g_1(z_1,x_1),g_2(z_2,x_2),\ldots,g_n(z_n,x_n)),$$

where x_i is the projection of $\varphi(z_1,z_2,\ldots,z_n,x)$ on the i-th coordinate. As special cases we can obtain some known operations. For instance, if we have two automata and choose

$$\varphi(z_1,z_2,x) = (x,f_1(z_1,x)), \quad \psi(z_1,z_2,x) = f_2(z_2,f_1(z_1,x)),$$

then we obtain the substitution.
Let R be a partial order on $\{1,2,\dots,n\}$. Then the product $\mathcal{A}$ of $\mathcal{A}_1, \mathcal{A}_2, \dots, \mathcal{A}_n$ is called an R-product if φ can be given in the form

$$\varphi(z_1,z_2,\dots,z_n,x) = (\varphi_1(z_1,\dots,z_n,x),\dots,\varphi_n(z_1,\dots,z_n,x))$$

and the functions φ_i, $i = 1,2,\dots,n$, do not essentially depend on z_j with $j < i$ (with respect to the order R). If $1 > 2$, then the superposition is an R-product. Obviously, feedback cannot be modelled by an R-product.
The Huzino product of the automata $\mathcal{A}_1 = (X, Z, g_1)$ and $\mathcal{A}_2 = (X, Z, g_2)$ with the same input set, the same set of states, and without outputs is given by the automaton $\mathcal{A} = (X, Z, g)$ where

$$g(z,x) = g_2(g_1(z,x),x).$$

We now define some completeness concepts with respect to the operations introduced above and give the associated results without proofs, which can be found in /GP/, /Gl/, /Hu/. In all cases, let M be a set of automata without initial states (and also without outputs if the Huzino product is considered).
M is called isomorphically complete if, for any sequential function F there are automata $\mathcal{A}_1, \mathcal{A}_2, \dots, \mathcal{A}_n$ in M (they need not be different) and functions φ and ψ such that the product of $\mathcal{A}_1, \mathcal{A}_2, \dots, \mathcal{A}_n$ with respect to φ and ψ has a Z-subautomaton which is isomorphic to an automaton which induces F by some state (as initial state).

<u>Theorem 7.14.</u> A set of automata is isomorphically complete if and only if it contains an automaton $\mathcal{A} = (X, Y, Z, g, f)$ which has two different states z, z' and input symbols $x_1,x_2,x_3,x_4 \in X$ such that

$$g(z,x_1) = z, \quad g(z,x_2) = z', \quad g(z',x_3) = z, \quad g(z',x_4) = z' .$$

Note, f is of no importance. This happens since ψ can be arbitrarily choosen.

<u>Corollary 7.15.</u> There is a finite isomorphically complete set.

<u>Corollary 7.16.</u> It is decidable whether or not a finite set of automata is isomorphically complete.

M is called R-complete iff, for any sequential function F, there are automata $\mathcal{A}_1, \mathcal{A}_2, \dots, \mathcal{A}_n \in M$ such that F is induced by a state (as initial state) of the S-product of $\mathcal{A}_1, \mathcal{A}_2, \dots, \mathcal{A}_n$, where S is a partial order on $\{1,2,\ldots,n\}$.

Theorem 7.17. There exist no finite R-complete sets of automata.

Again, we can introduce the metric of paragraph 5.1. and the metric R-completeness.

Theorem 7.18. There is a finite metrically R-complete set.

These results correspond to Theorem 4.5. and Theorem 5.1. (via Theorem 5.2.).
Let X and Z be fixed, finite, nonempty sets, which are the input set and state set, respectively, of all considered automata. M is called Huzino-complete iff any automaton $\mathcal{A} = (X, Z, g)$ can be obtained by iterated applications of the Huzino product to the automata of M.

Theorem 7.19. For arbitrary (fixed) X and Z, there is a Huzino-complete set which consists of two elements.

Evidently, the Huzino-completeness is decidable since we can construct the closure of a set (with respect to the Huzino product) in a finite number of steps.

Exercises

1. Prove that the set of all subalgebras of $\underline{Q_2}$ has the cardinality $\mathfrak{c}$.
2. Let k be a prime number. Prove that, for $j \geq 0$,

   $$Z_j = \{(f,d) : f(x,x,\ldots,x) = x + s \bmod k,\ d = k^j r,\ r \equiv s \mod k \text{ for some } s \in E_k\}$$

   is d_2-precomplete in Q_k (cf. /MRR/,/Ku1/).
3. Prove : If $id \in M$, then $M' = \{(f,1) : f \in M\}$ is d_2-complete if and only if M is complete in $\underline{P_k'}$.
4. We proved the u-precompleteness of some sets via a completeness criterion. Give a direct proof of the u-precompleteness of $K(a,b)$ and N, where $\underline{N}$ is maximal in $\underline{P_k'}$.
5. $M \subseteq Q_k$ is called fully complete iff, for any $f \in P_k'$, there is an integer d such that $(f,t) \in [M]_d$ for all $t \geq d$. Prove that M is fully complete if and only if M^+ is complete in $\underline{P_k'}$ and there are (id,d_1) and (id,d_2) in $[M]_d$ for two relatively prime numbers d_1 and d_2 (cf. /MRR/).

6. Prove that $\underline{V}_o$, $\underline{V}_1$, $\underline{V}_2$, $\underline{V}_3$, $\underline{V}_4$, $\underline{V}_5$ are subalgebras of $\underline{W}_2$.

7. Does there exist a set of two functions which is complete in $\underline{W}_2$?

8. Show that the set of all subalgebras of $\underline{W}_2$ has the cardinality $\mathfrak{c}$ (cf. /Ce3/).

9. We say that $M \subseteq P_k'$ is a separating set iff, for any $n \in \mathbb{N}$ and any set $S \subseteq E_k{}^n$, there are a function $f \in P_k'$ and a set $Y \subset E_k$ such that $f(a_1, a_2, \ldots, a_n) \in Y$ if and only if $(a_1, a_2, \ldots, a_n) \in S$.
   i) Prove that a subalgebra $\underline{R}$ of $\underline{P_k'}$ is separating if and only if M_R is a Kleene-set in P_k.
   ii) Study separating subalgebras.
   (Cf. /Da5/.)

BIBLIOGRAPHICAL AND HISTORICAL NOTES

First the completeness problem was considered in P_k'. There are three sources for these investigations:
- the propositional calculus of logic,
- the study of combinational circuits,
- the study of polynomials in universal algebras (a survey of results related to this approach is contained in /We/).

In 1920 E.L.Post (/Po/) determined all subalgebras of P_2' and obtained the completeness criterion using the maximal subalgebras (Theorem 3.5.). A modern presentation of these results is given in /JGK/. The finiteness of the number of maximal subalgebras was independently proved by A.V.Kuznecov (1951) and J.W.Butler (1960). The exact determination of the maximal subalgebras of P_k' is due to S.V.Jablonskij for $k = 3$ (1953, /Ja1/), A.I.Malcev for $k = 4$, and I.Rosenberg for arbitrary $k \geq 2$ (1965, /Ro1/, /Ro2/). The characterization of functions generating P_k' was given by V.B.Kudrjavcev (/Ku6/) and G.Rousseau (/Rou/). Summaries of the most important results on P_k' can be found in /Pö/, /Ro3/, /JL/, /Ja2/, /DDT/.
It has already been mentioned soon that $\underline{P_2}$ is finitely generated (e.g. /BW/ and the paper of Minsky in /SM/). The first example of a sequential function generating P_2 was given in /Ku1/. Then V.B.Kudrjavcev and V.A.Buevic gave simpler functions of this type, and finally Buevic proved the existence of an $F \in P_k^2$ with weight 2, whose closure is P_k (/Bu1/, /Bu2/).
The results on s-completeness (especially Theorem 4.10.) are due to S.V.Alesin, who considered in his dissertation some further interesting classes of automata (with infinite input alphabet and/or infinite set of states) with respect to their systems of generators (see /Al3/ and /KAP/).
In /Ho/ J.Horejs proved that the semigroup $\underline{P_k}^1$ is not finitely generated and, independently, F.Gecseg (/Ge2/) and V.P.Zarovnij (/Za/) showed that the group G_k of one-to-one mappings of P_k^1 has no finite system of generators. In his proof Zarovnij used the wreath product of groups, which gives some additional information (see also /GP/). Simultaneously, S.V.Alesin (/Al1/) and P.Dömösi (/Dö1/) proved that $\underline{P_k}^1$ and $\underline{G_k}$ are of type 2 (Theorem 6.3., Lemma 6.5.). Our proof follows the lines of /Dö1/.
In 1964 two essential contributions tothe completeness problem were made. Kudrjavcev (/Ku2/) showed that the set of maximal subalgebras of P_k has the cardinality $\mathfrak{c}$ (Theorem 4.14.) and M.I.Kratko (/Kr1/)

proved the undecidability of the completeness problem (Theorem 4.16.). Metric completeness was considered by B.Csakany, F.Gecseg (/CG/) and V.A.Buevic (/Bu3/, /Bu4/). The undecidability of m-completeness was shown by Buevic, and in /CG/it was proved that there is no finitely generated subsemigroup m-equivalent to P_k^1 or G_k and that there are irreducible sets whose closure is m-equivalent to P_k^1 and G_k, respectively. t-completeness was studied by Buevic in /Bu5/.

The Kleene-completeness was introduced and considered by the author (see /Da1/ - /Da10/). /Da11/ is a survey on the results. The material of the paragraphs 5.3., 5.4., 5.5. is taken from papers of Kratko, Kudrjavcev, and Alesin (/Kr2/, /Ku3/, /Al4/).

We mention two further modifications with a decidable completeness problem. Leticevskij (/Le/) investigated the case that the set M, which is under consideration, is given as $M = \widetilde{P_2} \cup M_1$ and proved a decidable sufficient and necessary condition for the completeness of M. B.Thalheim (/Th1/, /Th2/, /Th3/) investigated the restriction to t-stable automata (i.e. $g(z_0,p) = g(z_0,px)$ for $l(p) \geq t$, $x \in E_2$). He showed that it is decidable whether or not a finite set of t-stable automata generates all t-stable automata. This concept is closely related to t-completeness.

Here we note one of the most interesting open problems in this field: Find a concept of completeness such that any sequential function can be "almost generated" and the completeness problem is decidable. A special case is the following version: Find a metric such that the associated metric completeness is decidable.

The first paper on delayed functions was published by J.v.Neumann in /SM/. Independently, the d_1-completeness problem was solved by V.B.Kudrjavcev (/Ku1/) and L.Martin. The d_2-completeness problem in Q_2 was considered in /Ku1/. For $k \geq 3$, a description of d_2-precomplete sets was presented by A.Nozaki and his collegues (/HN/, /Hi/), other characterizations of some such sets were given in /MRR/. The d_2-completeness of subsets of Q_k^{+1} was studied by Nozaki. Our proof of Theorem 7.8. is taken from /No2/. /No3/ contains an exact determination of the u-precomplete sets for $k = 2,3$. d(1)-completeness is considered in /BK1/, and in /Bi1/, /Bi2/ the problem of d(r)-completeness is solved by L.A.Birjukova. The d_3-completeness is investigated in /BK2/. Further possible completeness concepts in Q_k are discussed in /Io/, especially motivated by practical aspects, /MRR/, and A.Nozaki (unpublished), where also general substitutions and feedback are allowed in some context.

The Ceitlin-algebra is studied in the papers /Ce2/, /Ce3/, /Ce4/ by G.E.Ceitlin (see also /GJC/). Note that there are no results on W_k, $k \geq 3$.

A summary of results on R-completeness and some of its modifications is given in /Dö2/.
In the monograph we have considered algebras whose underlying sets were formed by functions and the operations were $\zeta, \tau, \Delta, \nabla, \circ, \times$, and their modifications. This type of algebras was introduced by A.I.Malcev in /Mal/. He called such algebras iterative. There are also considered other algebraic problems. For congruence relations on P_k', P_k, and Q_k we refer to /La/ and /Da12/.

REFERENCES

/Ad/ S.I.Adian, The Burnside Problem and Identities in Groups. Berlin, 1979.

/Al1/ S.V.Alesin (С.В.Алёшин), Об отсутсвии базисов в некоторых классах инициальных автоматов. Пробл. кибернетики 22, 67-74 (1970).

/Al2/ -, Конечные автоматы и проблема Бернсайда о периодических группах. Мат. заметки 2, 319-328 (1972).

/Al3/ -, Относительно суперпозиций автоматных отображений. Диссертация, Москва, 1973.

/Al4/ -, Об одном критерии полноты для суперпозиций автоматных отображений. Rostock. Math. Colloq. 3, 119-132 (1977).

/Ar/ M.A.Arbib (Ed.), Algebraic Theory of Machines, Languages, and Semigroups. New York, 1968.

/ANT/ T.F.Arnold, M.M.Newburn, and C.J.Tau, Iteratively realized sequential circuits. Proc. Symp. Switching and Automata Theory, 431-448 (1968).

/Bi1/ L.A.Birjukova (Л.А.Бирюкова), Вопросы 1 -полноты для функций с задержками. Пробл. кибернетики 31, 53-75 (1976).

/Bi2/ -, Диссертация, Москва, 1977.

/BK1/ - and V.B.Kudrjavcev (- и В.Б.Кудрявцев), О полноте функции с задержками. Пробл. кибернетики 23, 5-25 (1970).

/BK2/ - and -, Некоторые задачи о полноте для функции с задержками. Исследование операций 4, 88-102 (1974).

/BBK/ G.N.Blochina, G.Burosch und V.B.Kudrjavcev, Ein Vollständigkeitskriterium bis auf eine gewise Äquivalenzrelation für eine verallgemeinerte Postsche Algebra. Publ. Math. 20, 141-152 (1973).

/BC/ V.G.Bodnarchuk, and G.E.Ceitlin (В.Г.Боднарчук и Г.Е.Цейтлин), Об алгебрах периодически определенных преобазований бесконечного регистра. Кибернетика 1, 18-27 (1969).

/Bu1/ V.A.Buevic (В.А.Буевич), Построение универсальной о.-д. функции от двух входных переменных. Пробл. кибернетики 15, (1965)

/Bu2/ -, Построение универсальной о.-д. функции от двух входных переменных, имеющей два внутренних состояния. Пробл. кибернетики 22, 75-83 (1970).

/Bu3/ -, Об алгоритмической неразрешимости распознавания A-полноты для ограниченно-детерминированных функций. Мат. зам. 11,(1972)

/Bu4/ -, Об аппрокцимационной полноте (A-полноте) автоматов. Диссертация, Москва, 1973.

/Bu5/ -, О τ-полноте в классе автоматных отображений. Докл. акад. наук 252, 1037-1041 (1980) (a complete version will appear in Пробл. кибернетики).

/BW/ A.Burks and J.Wright, Theory of logical nets. Proc. IRE 41, 10, 1357-1365 (1953).

/BDHL/ G.Burosch, J.Dassow, W.Harnau und D.Lau, Über Algebren von Prädikaten. Preprint, Wilhelm-Pieck-Universität Rostock, 1977 (to appear in Пробл. кибернетики).

/Ce1/ G.E.Ceitlin (Г.Е.Цейтлин), О критериях для конечной порождений в универсальных алгебрах. Кибернетика 3, 46-51 (1974).

/Ce2/ -, Вопросы функциональной полноты для одной модификаций алгебры логики. Кибернетика 4, 39-44 (1969).

/Ce3/ -, Структура модифицированной алгебры Поста и ее свойства. Кибернетика 4, 39-54 (1970).

/Ce4/ -, О бесконечно порожденных подалгебрах модифицированной алгебры Поста. Кибернетика 2, 43-55 (1971).

/Co/ P.M.Cohn, Universal Algebra. New York, 1965.

/CEW/ I.M.Copi, C.C.Elgot, and J.B.Wright, Realization of events by logical nets. JACM 5, 181-196 (1958).

/Coy/ W.Coy, Universelle Klassen O(log(M×N))-testbarer iterativer und sequentieller Schaltungen. 5.Jahrestagg. Gesellsch. f. Informatik LNCS 34, 534-544 (1975).

/CG/ B.Csakany and F.Gecseg, О группе автоматных подстановок. Кибернетика 5, 14-17 (1965).

/Da1/ J.Dassow, Kleene-Mengen und Kleene-Vollständigkeit. EIK 10, 287-295 (1974).

/Da2/ -, Kleene-Vollständigkeit bei stark-definiten Ereignissen. EIK 10, 399-405 (1974).

/Da3/ -, Über zwei abgeschlossene Mengen von Automatenoperatoren. Wiss. Zeitschr. d. Univ. Rostock, Math-Nat. Reihe 23, 763-767 (1974).

/Da4/ -, Über metrische Kleene-Vollständigkeit. EIK 11, 557-560 (1975).

/Da5/ -, Kleene-Mengen und trennende Mengen. Math. Nachr. 74, 89-97 (1976)

/Da6/ -, Einige Bemerkungen zu einem modifizierten Vollständigkeitsbegriff für Automatenabbildungen. Rostock. Math. Kolloq. 3, 69-84 (1977).

/Da7/ -, Some remarks on the algebra of automaton mappings. Proc. Symp. Fundamentals of Comput. Theory, LNCS 56, 78-83 (1977).

/Da8/ -, Some remarks on the algebra of automata. Proc. Conf. Operat. Syst., Közl. - MTA SztAKI Budapest 87/1978, 71-78 (1978).

/Da9/ -, Einige Bemerkungen über einstellige sequentielle Funktionen. Submitted for publication.

/Da10/ -, Pre-Kleene-sets. Submitted for publication.

/Da11/ -, Ein modifizierter Vollständigkeitsbegriff in einer Algebra von Automatenabbildungen. Dissertation, Rostock, 1978.

/Da12/ -, On the congruence lattice of algebras of automaton mappings. Proc. Colloq. Finite Algebras and Multiple-Valued Logic, 1979, to appear.

/DDT/ M.Davio, J.P.Deschamps, and A.Thayse, Discrete and Switching Functions. St. Saphorin, New York, 1978.

/Dö1/ P.Dömösi, On the semigroup of automaton mappings with finite alphabet. Acta Cybernetica 1, 251-254 (1972).

/Dö2/ -, On product of finite automata. In preparation.

/Ei/ E.Eichelberger, Hazard detection in combinational and sequential circuits. IBM J. Res. Develop. 9, 90-99 (1965).

/Ge1/ F.Gecseg, On R-products of automata I, II, III. Studia Sci. Math. Hung. 1, 437-441; 443-447 (1966); 2, 163-166 (1967).

/Ge2/ -, О группе взаимно однозначных преобразований, определенных конечными автоматами. Кибернетика 1, 37-39 (1965).

/GP/ - and I.Peak, Algebraic Theory of Automata. Budapest, 1972.

/Gl/ W.M.Gluschkow, Theorie der abstrakten Automaten. Berlin, 1963.

/GJC/ -, G.E.Ceitlin, and E.L.Juscenko (В.М.Глушков, Г.Е.Цейтлин и Е.Л.Ющенко), Алгебра, языки, программирование. Киев, 1974.

/Go/ E.S.Golod (Е.С.Голод), О ниль-алгебрах и финитно-аппроксимируемых группах. Изв. АН СССР, сер. мат. 28, 273-276 (1964).

/Gö/ W.Görke, Fehlerdiagnose digitaler Schaltungen. Stuttgart, 1973.

/Hal/ M.Hall (jr), The Theory of Groups. New York, 1959.

/HS/ J.Hartmanis and R.E.Stearns, Algebraic Structure Theory of Sequential Machines. Prentice-Hall, 1966.

/Hay/ J.P.Hayes, On the realization of Boolean functions requiring a minimal or near-minimal number of tests. IEEE Trans. Comput. C-20, 1506-1513 (1971).

/He/ O.Herzog, Zwei zellulare Netzwerke zur Realisierung Boolescher Funktionen. Preprint, GMD Bonn, Nr. 52, 1972.

/Hi/ T.Hikita, Completeness criteria for delayed-logic devices. Preprint, Univ. Tokyo.

/HN/ - and A.Nozaki, A completeness criterion for spectra. SIAM J. Comput. 6, 285-297 (1977).

/Ho/ J.Horejs, Durch endliche Automaten definierte Abbildungen. Probl. d. Kybernetik 6, 31-35 (1966).

/Hu/ S.Huzino, On the existence of Sheffer stroke class in the sequential machines. Mem. Fac. Sci. Kyushu Univ., Ser. A 13, 52-68 (1959).

/Ja1/ S.V.Jablonskij (С.В.Яблонский) , Функциональные построение в к-значной логике. Тр. мат. ин-та АН СССР 51, 5-142 (1958).

/Ja2/ -, Введение в дискретную математику. Москва, 1979.

/JGK/ -, G.P.Gawrilow und W.B.Kudrjawzew, Boolesche Funktionen und Postsche Klassen. Berlin, 1970.

/JL/ - und O.B.Lupanov (Ed.), Diskrete Mathematik und mathematische Fragen der Kybernetik. Berlin, 1980.

/Jac/ J.Jaczewski, Logical Systems for Industrial Applications. Warszawa, Amsterdam, 1978.

/Kl/ C.C.Kleene, Introduction to Metamathematics. Amsterdam, 1967.

/KT/ N.E.Kobrinski und B.A.Trachtenbrot, Einführung in die Theorie der endlichen Automaten. Berlin, 1967.

/Kr1/ M.I.Kratko (М.И.Кратко) , Алгоритмическая нерасрешимость проблемы распознавания полноты для конечных автоматов. Докл. акад. наук 155, 35-37 (1964).

/Kr2/ -, Алгоритмическая неразрешимость одной задачи из теории конечных автоматов. Дискретный анализ 2, 37-41 (1964).

/Ku1/ V.B.Kudrjavcev (В.Б.Кудрявцев) , Теорема полноты для одного класса автоматов бес обратных связей. Пробл. кибернетики 8, 91-115 (1962).

/Ku2/ –, О мощностях множеств предполных множеств некоторых функциональных систем связанных с автоматами. Пробл. кибернетики 13, 45-74 (1965).

/Ku3/ –, О функциональных свойствах логических сетей. Math. Nachr. 55, 187-211 (1973).

/Ku4/ –, Диссертация, Rostock, 1973.

/Ku5/ –, Лекции по теории конечных автоматов. Москва, 1976.

/Ku6/ –, О свойствах S-систем функций k- значной логики. EIK 9, 81-105 (1973).

/KAP/ –, S.V.Alesin, and A.S.Podkolsin (–, С.В.Алешин и А.С.Подкользин), Элементы теории автоматов. Москва, 1978.

/La/ D.Lau, Congruence relations on closed sets of multiple-valued logic. Proc. Colloq. Finite Algebras and Multiple-Valued Logic, 1979, to appear.

/Le/ A.A.Leticevskij (А.А.Летичевский), Условия полноты в классе автоматов Мура. Материалы научных семинаров по теорет. и приклад. вопросам кибернетики 2, 1-39 (1963).

/Lo/ H.H.Loomis (jr.), Completeness of sets of delayed-logic devices. IEEE Trans. Electron. Comput. EC-14, 157-172 (1965).

/Mal/ A.I.Malcev (А.И.Мальцев), Итеративные алгебры и многообразия Поста. Алгебра и логика 5, 5-24 (1966).

/Ma/ A.A.Markov (А.А.Марков), Теория алгоритмов. Тр. мат. ин-та АН СССР 42, 1954.

/MRR/ L.Martin, C.Reischer, and I.Rosenberg, Completeness problems for switching circuits constructed from delayed gates. Proc. 8th Internat. Symp. Multiple-Valued Logic, 1-10, 1978.

/Mi/ R.E.Miller, Switching Theory. Vol. 1: Combinatorial circuits, Vol. 2: Sequential circuits. New York, 1965.

/No1/ A.Nozaki, Complete sets of switching elements and related topics. First USA-Japan Comput. Conf. 393-396, 1972.

/No2/ –, Functional completeness of multi-valued logical functions under uniform composition. Rep. Fac. Engineerg. Yamanashi Univ. 29, 61-67 (1978).

/No3/ –, Maximal $\varkappa$ - incomplete sets of functions defined over the set $\{0,1,2\}$. Preprint, 1979.

/No4/ –, Practical decomposition of automata. Inform. Control 36, 275-291 (1978)

/Po/ E.L.Post, Introduction to a general theory of elementary propositions. Amer. J. Math. 43, 163-185 (1921).

/Pö/ R.Pöschel und A.Kaluznin, Funktionen- und Relationen-Algebren. Ein Kapitel der diskreten Mathematik. Berlin, 1979.

/Re/ S.Reddy, Easily testable realizations for logic functions. IEEE Trans. Comput. C-21, 1183-1188 (1972).

/Ro1/ I.Rosenberg, La structure des fonctions de plusier variables sur un ensemble fini. C. R. Acad. Sci. Paris Groupe 5, 3817-3819 (1965).

/Ro2/ -, Über die funktionale Vollständigkeit in den mehrwertigen Logiken. Rozpr. CSAV Rada Mat. Prir. Ved. Praha 80, 3-93 (1970)

/Ro3/ -, Completeness properties of multiple-valued logic algebras. In: D.C.Rine (Ed.), Computer Science and Multiple-Valued Logic. Amsterdam, 1977, 144-186.

/Rou/ G.Rousseau, Completeness in finite algebras with a single operation. Proc. Amer. Math. Soc. 18, 1009-1013 (1967).

/Sa/ A.Salomaa, Some completeness criterion for sets of functions over a finite domain I, II. Turun Yliopiston Julkaisuja Ann. Univ. Turkuensis A 53, 1-9 (1962); 63, 1-19 (1963).

/SM/ C.E.Shannon and J.McCarthy (Ed.), Automata Sudies. Princeton, 1956.

/St/ P.Starke, Abstrakte Automaten. Berlin, 1969.

/Th1/ B.Thalheim, О решетках замкнутых классов стабильных автоматов. Методы и системы техн. диагностики 1 , Саратов, 1979.

/Th2/ -, Условия полноты и выразимости для стабильных автоматов. Диссертация, Москва, 1979.

/Th3/ -, Über ein Vollständigkeitskriterium für eine Klasse von Automaten (einstellige Approximationsautomaten). To appear in Rostock. Math. Kolloq.

/Tr1/ B.A.Trachtenbrot (Б.А.Трахтенброт) , Осложности схем, реализующих многопараметрические семейства операторов. Пробл. кибернетики 12, 99-112 (1964).

/Tr2/ -, Algorithmen und Rechenautomaten. Berlin, 1977.

/Un/ S.Unger, Hazards and delays in asynchronous sequential switching circuits. Trans. Circuit Th. CT-6, 12-25 (1959).

/We/ H.Werner, Discriminator-Algebras. Studien zur Algebra und ihrer Anwendungen. Bd. 6, Berlin, 1978.

/Za/ V.P.Zarovnij (В.П.Заровный), Автоматные подстановки и сплетения групп. Кибернетика 1, 29-36 (1965).

INDEX

Bei Fragen zur Produktsicherheit wenden Sie sich bitte an:
If you have any questions regarding product safety,
please contact:

Walter de Gruyter GmbH
Genthiner Straße 13
10785 Berlin
productsafety@degruyterbrill.com